WORKS OF BERTOLT BRECHT

The Grove Press Edition

General Editor: Eric Bentley

Translators

Lee Baxandall

Eric Bentley

Martin Esslin

H. R. Hays

Christopher Isherwood

Frank Jones

Charles Laughton

Carl R. Mueller

Desmond I. Vesey

WORKS BY BERTOLT BRECHT

PUBLISHED BY GROVE PRESS

Baal, A Man's A Man, and The Elephant Calf

The Caucasian Chalk Circle

Edward II: A Chronicle Play

Galileo

The Good Woman of Setzuan

The Jewish Wife and Other Short Plays
(In Search of Justice, The Informer, The Elephant Calf,
The Measures Taken, The Exception and the Rule,
Salzburg Dance of Death)

Jungle of Cities and Other Plays
(Drums in the Night, Roundheads and Peakheads)

Manual of Piety

The Mother

Mother Courage and Her Children

Parables for the Theater

Selected Poems

Seven Plays
(Galileo, Saint Joan of the Stockyards, In the Swamp,
A Man's A Man, Mother Courage, The Good Woman of Setzuan,
The Caucasian Chalk Circle)

Threepenny Novel

The Threepenny Opera

The Visions of Simone Machard (with Lion Feuchtwanger)

THE MOTHER

BERTOLT BRECHT

THE MOTHER

With Notes by the Author

Translated and with an Introduction by

LEE BAXANDALL

GROVE PRESS
NEW YORK

The name Grove Press and the colophon printed on the title page and outside of this book are trademarks registered in the U.S. Patent and Trademark Office and in other countries.

Published by Grove Press
a division of Wheatland Corporation
841 Broadway
New York, N.Y. 10003

Library of Congress Cataloging-in-Publication Data

Brecht, Bertolt, 1898-1956
    The Mother.
    Based on the novel Mat' by M. Gor'kii.
    I. Gor'kii, Maksim, 1868-1936. Mat'. II. Title
[PT2603.R397M793   1978b]   832'.9'12   65-14211

First Black Cat Edition 1965
First Evergreen Edition 1989
ISBN 0-8021-3160-3

Manufactured in the United States of America

This book is printed on acid-free paper.

The Mother was written in the style of a *Lehrstück* ("play for learning"), although it requires professional actors. The play's dramaturgy is antimetaphysical, materialistic and NON-ARISTOTELIAN. Thus it declines to assist the spectator in *surrendering himself to empathy* in the unthinking fashion of the Aristotelian dramaturgy; and it relates to certain psychic effects, as for instance catharsis, in an essentially different manner. In the same way as it refuses to tacitly hand over its heroes to the world as though to an inalterable destiny, it also has no intention of handing over the spectator to a "suggestive" theater experience. Rather its concern is to teach the spectator a most definitely practical conduct that is intended to change the world, and for this reason he must be afforded a fundamentally different attitude in the theater from that to which he is habituated.

—From Brecht's Notes to *The Mother*

Introduction

This play was begun by Brecht in 1930 and completed the next year.[1] The idea and general outlines were taken from the novel, *Mother,* which Maxim Gorki wrote in the Adirondacks in 1906 while in America to collect funds and swing public opinion behind the Russian revolutionists in the aftermath of the Tsar's Bloody Sunday.

The novel gained world fame and was several times adapted for stage and screen, perhaps most effectively by Pudovkin in 1926. Ready to Brecht's hand was the draft of yet another adaptation, this one for the Berlin Volksbühne.[2] Brecht often worked from drafts, translations, or scenarios of others, assimilating them to his own style and viewpoint.

A "collective," as he liked to term friends who assisted, was involved in the work. The printed edition mentions Günther Weisenborn, a collaborator on the Volksbühne version, Hanns Eisler, the composer and Schoenberg pupil who had written, with Brecht, numerous militant songs and *The Measures Taken* (1930), and Slatan Dudow, a young Bulgarian with experience at Piscator's theater. In 1932 this same team joined with Ernst Ottwalt to make *Kuhle Wampe,* a film no less controversial than *The Mother.*

On January 17, 1932, at the Theatre am Schiffbauerdamm, where Brecht's Berlin Ensemble performs today, *The Mother* was first presented to the public. In 1919 on this same day Rosa Luxemburg, then the leading woman

---

1. The present text is a translation of Brecht's *Die Mutter,* published in *Versuche,* Heft 7 (1933).

2. By the *Dramaturg* at the Volksbühne, Günther Stark, with the writer Günther Weisenborn. A copy is in the Brecht-Archiv, Berlin. Excerpts may be seen in Werner Mittenzwei, *Bertolt Brecht,* Aufbau: Berlin, 1962, 73-75.

revolutionary of Germany, was murdered with Karl Lieb-knecht by the police who had them in custody. A few days after their deaths Brecht attended a protest meeting convened by the Augsburg Soviet. He also composed a "Ballad of the Red Rosa." The opening of *The Mother* was timed to fall on this anniversary.

The clean, sparse stage design with projected backdrops was the work of Caspar Neher, who grew up with Brecht and worked frequently with him while gaining such fame that the New York Metropolitan Opera has employed him. Eisler possibly never composed a better, more lively, or tuneful score. Pelagea Vlassova was played by Helene Weigel, Brecht's wife. Ernst Busch took the role of Pavel. The playwright directed.[3]

Eventually *The Mother* was taken to halls and clubs in the workers' districts of Berlin. It was Brecht's last play to reach performance before the advent of Hitler who ended the staging of *The Mother* with all Brecht's other works. Yet the play was produced on at least two other occasions before World War II. An amateur group, the Copenhagen Revolutionary Theatre, performed it while Brecht and his entourage were in Denmark in 1935. Theatre Union of New York also staged *The Mother* in November, 1935, with the author on hand.

Theatre Union was a left-wing professional company begun the year before with the intention of appealing to labor unions. Through this entry Brecht appears to have hoped to gain New World partisans for the epic theater. The opportunity seemed there. After Theatre Union staged Friedrich Wolf's *Sailors of Cattaro* its author had declared:

---

3. Settings and music were important to the play's effectiveness. The music is available on 78 or 45 rpm Eterna records and may be ordered from Deutscher Buch-Export und -Import GmbH., Leipzig C 1, Talstr. 29. Neher's designs are in *Theaterarbeit,* ed. Ruth Berlau et al, Dresden, 1952.

"The Left New York Theatre today . . . is without exaggeration the strongest and most outstanding outpost of the Left Theatre in all the capitalist countries."[4]

All the same, Brecht shortly found himself caught in a round of controversies. Theatre Union had its own strong ideas on presenting the conversion of Vlassova to Communism. This organization's financial situation and methods of work, as well as its ideas, left small latitude for the difficult innovations of a foreign playwright—who, it may be added, was hardly known here. (An extensive search of the chief cultural Communist organs for the U.S.—*Partisan Review, New Masses, New Theatre,* and *International Literature*—failed to reveal mention of Brecht prior to his debarkation here, save for oblique reference in articles devoted to Hanns Eisler and a severe review by Alfred Kurella of *The Measures Taken,* all in the latter journal, which was published in Moscow. These publications had meanwhile tended to make heroes of such figures as Wolf, Eisler, Erich Mühsam, Willi Bredel, Hans Marchwitza, Ludwig Renn, Anna Seghers, and Johannes Becher.)

Perhaps more fundamental than Brecht's lack of prestige and his artistic and temperamental differences with the Theatre Union[5] was the basic change of world Communist policy which occurred even as *The Mother* was picked and prepared for New York production. The task of the hour in Communist eyes was now to rally men of good will *of all classes* against Hitler. With the so-called People's Front policies thus launched, *The Mother* scarcely could have proved less apt for Theatre Union purposes.

Nevertheless, Paul Peters went ahead with his transla-

---

4. For more on Theatre Union, see Gerald Rabkin, *Drama and Commitment,* Indiana University Press: Bloomington, 1964, 45-70.

5. Brecht's account of the differences is in *Brecht on Theatre,* John Willett, ed., Hill & Wang: New York, 1964, 81-84.

tion and with an adaptation,[6] and Brecht was asked to come. The screen director Joseph Losey reports watching Brecht stalk from a rehearsal of *The Mother* with the outraged shout: *Dreck!* Adjustment to the People's Front stylistic norms and viewpoint clearly was difficult for him; as early as the June, 1935 Paris International Congress of Writers, he reminded an audience (in a speech that Communist journals failed to print) that fascism's economic origins were being overlooked.[7]

The Mother at the Theatre Union received mostly unfavorable or hostile notices from the Left press. It survived only thirty-six performances; had Theatre Union not had subscription audiences, the play might have closed sooner. A curtain of silence and embarrassment dropped over the incident. Nor would the Left press publish Brecht's defense of the play. When he embarked for Scandinavia in early 1936 Brecht's hopes of establishing his drama in this "strongest and most outstanding outpost of Left Theatre in all the capitalist countries" lay in ruins. He was to describe this experience with disgust such as is betrayed for no other staging calamity in his career. When, with the outbreak of total war, Brecht did return to America in 1941 he settled, not on the East coast, but in California.

The Mother has since been performed at Halle, Leipzig, Havana, and elsewhere; most important for our grasping its importance to the author, Brecht chose to include *The Mother* among the works that provided the foundation of his Berlin Ensemble repertory. In 1951 he personally staged it, close upon productions of *Mother Courage* and *Puntila*. Ernst Busch and Helene Weigel were again in leading roles. After Brecht's death this production was reworked by Manfred Wekwerth. DEFA, the East German film administration, preserved it for the future.

---

6. Both Peters versions are in the Theater Collection of the New York Public Library.

7. The speech can be found in his *Versuche,* Heft 15.

Of all the complex dramatic figures Brecht conceived in his Marxist period (1929-1956), Vlassova the Mother stands out as *the one near-totally positive* character. More than that, she is not stupid, lecherous, philistine, or a combination of these qualities. She is intelligent and above all, she is a *motherly* woman, where his earlier females without exception were the sexual toys of more powerful male personalities or, if independently powerful, grotesque and crude. With Vlassova for the first time the problems of a woman become Brecht's sphere of main concern. An evident enlargement of his sympathies and ethical thought was involved.

Brecht settled upon woman in her social role as the best protagonist available for the thorough exploration of moral situations. In his earlier works, young men had made the tough decisions how to live. From *The Mother* on it is chiefly heroines who face the agonizing choices. The reason for this is to be found in the root Brechtian ethical criterion. Again and again it is defined in his plays from the late twenties on. Brecht's moral code, simple enough and practical enough to be studied in action, readily verified or disproved as to results, and quite impossible to live up to entirely under prevalent conditions, asks: *Do you work and plan to fulfill other humans' needs, desires, and potential wherever met?*

To Brecht's view, women live most near to, and we can say, desperately with this imperative. Their children are the hope of the next generations. Thus whether coming generations will find their human potential fulfilled depends more than anything upon whether women will resolutely and resourcefully meet the full range of child needs. But these women were once children. Their inadequacy as the fulfillers of child potential may be traced in large part to what as children they did not receive. Then too, women face a more pressing responsibility in the child-raising burden than do men; this fact generally relegates women to an exploited role in relations with men, further impairing their ability to rise fully to the moral demands of maternity. The cycle, mother and child, is therefore both marvelous and discouraging but surely the root human relationship is there.

Brecht chose with *The Good Woman of Setzuan* to emphasize the most severe or terrible aspects of woman's ethical role. Because Shen Te has had a little unexpected luck which led her in turn to give herself unreservedly to love, she is forced into the prospect of becoming a mother. The outlook is that she is to become hopelessly dependent and ruthlessly exploited. The alternative is that she can decide to become Shui Ta; decide, that is, to develop in her own person as the exploiter. She poses the dilemma to three visiting gods. These, because they lack confidence that the world might be made better, precipitately flee, pausing only to urge moderation upon the "good" woman when, as they foresee she will and must, she exploits her fellow.

By contrast, *The Caucasian Chalk Circle* stresses the possibility that motherhood affords for the improvement of man's condition. A child, abandoned to almost certain death by its authentic, blood mother, is awarded by a judge to the custody of Grusha, a woman who rescued and took good care of it for several years. A narrator describes an explicit connection between morality and the realization of potentials:

> What there is shall go to those who are good for it,
> Thus: the children to the motherly, that they prosper
> The carts to good drivers, that they are driven well
> And the valley to the waterers, that it bring forth fruit.

The fulfilling of potential implies, however, some perspective on tomorrow. Without such outlook the murky omnipresence of Now is engulfing; while if one *can* spot potential, a mandate should likewise be sensed, urging one to act continuously on principles that will let down ladders from tomorrow.

In *The Mother* this gets its most sharp and explicit statement. Vlassova shapes her life by her expectations of what the Revolution will do for her kind and the final scene affirms the triumph of her morality:

> The victims of today will be victors of tomorrow
> And Never is changed into Today!

This mother, unlike the gentle Grusha, is a revolutionist. She chooses violent struggle—sensing no other choice, she would add—and her only son is taken in the cause her life affirms. Is this motherly conduct? Can Brecht reconcile the moral of *The Mother* with that in *The Caucasian Chalk Circle*?

Brecht does. Let us trace his thought by first getting firmly in mind what for Brecht were the essential traits of the women whom he thought maternal (maternal now being used as synonymous with "moral" or "useful to human needs and potential").

The women who for Brecht qualified as motherly types, more or less selflessly disposed to actions of use to others include Vlassova, Grusha, Shen Te, Kattrin (*Mother Courage*), Joan Dark, Simone Machard, Señora Carrar, Anna II (*Seven Deadly Sins*).

By contrast, a list of women with little or no inclination to take risks that help others include Courage, Widow Begbick, Mrs. Mi Tsu and Mrs. Yang (*The Good Woman of Setzuan*), Anna I, Natella Abashwili and Aniko Vashnadze (*The Caucasian Chalk Circle*).

Fairly consistent traits distinguish the first group from the second. The only woman in her city who "can't say no" is Shen Te. The only woman in the panicky palace who bothers about an abandoned infant is Grusha. She takes it to safety without thinking of the burden it will prove to be. The *motherly* person for Brecht generally displays such an impulsiveness, openness to experience, unusual energy, and disregard for the costs of responsibility.

These seem the minimal qualities that on Brecht's stage bring a person of eventual moral distinction into history.

Later, spontaneity may be buttressed with stony wisdom: when Vlassova knows her son dead in the struggle; when Grusha witnesses her marriage hopes grow remote because she has a child not even her own; when Simone awaits martyrdom. But—Brecht seems to argue—wisdom does not spur a person to generous conduct. Instinct moves him, or perhaps it is the glands and hormones coupled with childhood conditioning. But this dramatist who is the greatest admirer of human reason since Shaw makes clear his belief that reason is *not* ultimately what makes man moral. At best, he suggests, reason can arm the moral instinct. The irreducible test of who is motherly has to do with the person's energy and generosity of impulse. Although class and other social conditions shape and distort these traits, they are not in themselves *class-engendered*.[8]

Women can be divided then into the categories of the motherly and the barbarous, as Brecht often termed the immoral. The latter, characterized in general by their poverty of generous impulse, are recognizable above all by their failure to take long-range measures for the defense of their children and other near ones. The prime example is Mother Courage's ultimate indifference to the fate of her children.

Among the motherly there are two categories; when these are seen it will be grasped how Brecht can praise both

---

8. Marx in *The Holy Family* (1844) similarly describes Marie, the prostitute in Eugène Sue's *Les mystères de Paris* as a generous and outgoing "*natural* essence": "She is *good* because she is still *young,* full of hope and vitality. Her situation is *not good* because it does her unnatural violence, because it is not the expression of her human impulses, the fulfillment of her human desires. . . . In spite of her frailty *Fleur de Marie* shows great vitality, energy, cheerfulness, elasticity of character—qualities which alone explain her human development in her *inhuman* situation."—*The Holy Family*. Foreign Languages Publishing House, Moscow, 1956, pp. 225-227.

Vlassova and Grusha from a single ethical perspective, without bringing a flaw into his thought. Alone among Brecht's major heroines, Vlassova acts in both motherly manners in turn. She follows at first the time-hallowed course: she tries to remove her child from danger, by the same token doing all she can to save Pavel from his Bolshevik seducers. Similarly Grusha takes the noble infant to the far mountains. And Shen Te, become Shui Ta, on a basis of commercial exploitation, forms an enclave where her child may enjoy advantages such as the security she has not herself known. Each woman practices a form of *withdrawal,* the only recourse available to the timeless first category of mothers.

And within limits it is a useful strategy. Brecht often pays it tribute. But he demonstrates its limits as well. The humiliations heaped upon Grusha are shown. Shen Te's suffering whether she exploits or is exploited is shown. The words spoken to Grusha at her moment of choice, "Terrible is the temptation of goodness!" take on profound cautionary meaning. For to withdraw from trouble in Brecht's landscape often is not possible and never does it provide a permanent solution.

Motherliness, old style, costs too much—when an alternative is at hand. Vlassova at last must face the poor consequences of traditional motherly ways. Her son's salary is cut repeatedly and she cannot make the kopeks go further, try what she will. Step by step she is introduced to the new, revolutionary maternity. The heroine of the one-act *The Rifles of Señora Carrar* is drawn into the Spanish Civil War when the son she had meant to preserve from struggle is shot and killed while tranquilly at his fishing. Avoidance of trouble in this way gives place to confrontations with the unjust society by masses of people who think and organize in concert.

Nonetheless, Brecht apparently thought of the revolutionary morality to which he had come in much the same relativistic framework as he regarded the earlier ethics.

Either withdrawal from conflicts or taking an organized part in them might serve as an adequate response to a given historical situation. Brecht's great poem of 1938, "To Posterity," even shows that he would have *preferred* with-drawal from danger as a permanent ethic, had this only seemed appropriate:

> In old books is set down what wisdom is:
> To keep oneself from the world's strife and to pass
> One's brief time without fear
> To get along without violence,
> To return good for evil,
> Not to fulfill one's desires, but to forget them,
> These things are valued as wisdom.
> All of which is not possible for me;
> Truly I live in a dark age!

Thus Brecht came to laud Vlassova the Mother, Vlassova the Revolutionary.

From *The Mother* emerges also a view of how man learns. No more than he desired to produce wholly emotional experiences for audiences did Brecht desire the audience to witness a conversion tale that developed on wholly emotional grounds without a probing, checking, mediating role for the intellect.

He sought to bring out the basis in prevailing human relationships for the change of the Mother's mind. He strove to connect this basis in relationships with the actual structure of the Mother's recognition of "realities." For Brecht the learning experience, when not a credulous swallowing of nonsensical notions, consists of an active, audacious shuttling back and forth between ideas and practice with the latter confirming or modifying the ideas.

In this aspect *The Mother* perhaps can be understood best by contrast with some familiar, more conventional and non-Marxist examples of *Bildungsromanen* or narratives of an education.

At an opposite pole from *The Mother* are the novels *The Magic Mountain* by Thomas Mann and James Joyce's *A Portrait of the Artist as a Young Man*. Both of these narratives concern young men who, relatively speaking, are physically though not intellectually passive. Both listen with rapt attention to discourse, discourse, discourse, the one at an Alpine sanatorium and the other at a Jesuit school and around his family board. At last these young men emerge educated. What has been the process? They have listened! To a Marxist, and so to Brecht, such accounts of the making of a mind seem superficial and "idealist." The Marxist grants a relative independence to the shaping force of ideas. But this force has not been satisfactorily passed, in such narratives, through the medium of real relationships within the complex of social life; instead the ideas are hypothesized to have consequences, one imagines rather as radio waves are communicated.

In *The Mother* Brecht satirizes one such fellow who believes that ideas are formed as colds are caught, by the exposure to one or the other. The class to which the teacher Vessovchikov belongs gives him a vested interest in privileges of the existing order, as well as leisure and a certain remoteness from basic economic reality, so that the philosophizing in which he indulges for the benefit of his students is often verbosely prejudiced and ignorant. While it is true that he is badly paid, and his outlook is conducive to despair —factors that will dispose him to rethink his position once the workers' struggle has entered his experience—in the main the false consciousness of a bourgeois who is not happy, but lacks the necessary perspective to understand his anxiety, is exhibited beautifully in Vessovchikov. But while Brecht creates this figure for ridicule, his counterparts are produced by Joyce and Mann with no air of levity.

Vlassova chooses to influence the growth of this teacher's mind at the advanced stage of her own development. First, her own education must occur. How does it happen? Like many, she is reluctant to become involved in new experiences that may prove threatening; her home and kitchen abet this reluctance, they offer a sanctuary where advice learned at her mother's apron can remain beyond challenge. Her son makes these hopes vain. He has joined the Bolsheviks after daily exposure to the relations of production and to the winds of change that blow through his factory. His activities bring Vlassova from her kitchen.

Brecht gives us the Mother's thinking: her first new steps are taken for the old reasons, and for a time *she still functions according to the precept requiring that a mother keep her son out of trouble.* Thus one day she takes Pavel's place distributing leaflets at the factory, and sees men who read them arrested. But she has gone there simply so he will not; and she blames the leaflets, not the police, for the arrests. They must be bad leaflets, she thinks. But their content seems not so bad when explained to her. Yet the words of the son and his friends are not convincing; from the viewpoint Brecht has adopted, this was only to be expected. The hand of the past is strong. She has not seen enough. Vlassova is curious though and eager now to confirm her views. On impulse she joins the May Day demonstration and is present when unarmed workers are shot for demands that seem right to her. Now the floodgates of habituation collapse, and Marxist formulations which had meant nothing are suffused suddenly with meaning. They explain the nature of the factory system, from whence her living and her misery come.

The most perceptive comments on *The Mother* at its première were perhaps expressed by Walter Benjamin, a brilliant essayist and a friend of Brecht. He suggested that the play fundamentally was a "sociological experiment based upon the revolutionizing" of Vlassova. The Mother, he said, made one believe she was Marx's "*praxis* incarnate." While this is one way to sum up the education we have discussed, it should be added that the experiment on the Mother's mentality is in large part completed by the time she seeks haven with the teacher, rather early in the play. She will grow more shrewd, to be sure; she will lapse at times into doubt and sometimes into insensitivity. But her road is set and she will henceforth actively take her place among the agencies of social change.

She now becomes the sociologist and educator, applying to revolution the slyness which once she bent toward sheer survival. Her teaching methods are not mechanical in the least. Vlassova is aware that human consciousness is diverse, many-sided and hard to entice. She emerges as a master psychologist, the subtlety of her pedagogic approach the more manifest in comparison with such sterile sloganeering as the peasant Yegor practices, who stones her when she arrives in the country. Yegor talks in terms of laws of history while he fails to see possibilities in particular humans. He believes—in a manner recalling Vlassova's outgrown credulity for traditional maxims—that the "peasants are peasants and workers are workers" and never can join forces, while Vlassova promptly gives this notion the lie. Vlassova can measure the individual. She tailors her tactics to each occasion. Sometimes she directly exhorts but more often she turns common situations—a trip to the store, a conversation, a scrap collection or parade—slightly askew, making them appear odd and hopefully challenging, so bystanders who are already somewhat out of patience with inhumanity may perhaps be jarred to new awareness and, possibly, into action. Just in this way the butcher is made to join Yegor on strike. Meanwhile the portrayal of Yegor offers proof that Brecht learned early to reject the vulgar distortion of Marxism. "It is men who change circumstances," as Marx had said in the "Theses on Feuerbach"; "and the educator himself needs educating."

Vlassova seems in some part to embody the formative attitudes of her creator.

Brecht all his life wrote Herr Keuner stories, little anecdotes in which he sought the gist of his typical responses to situations. One Herr Keuner story seems to beg mention in view of the light it throws upon the Mother's—and presumably Brecht's—way of regarding people:

> Herr Keuner had little knowledge of human nature. He said, "You only need to know human nature when its exploitation is your object. *To think means to alter.* When I think of a person, I alter him at the same time; to me it almost seems he's not at all as he is, he only was so when I began to think of him."

In this way an extraordinary capacity to see man and the world in their developmental aspect is characteristic of the most positive of Brecht's figures. It seems in fact to have dominated Brecht's approach to writing and to associates, as we gather from numerous accounts of his procedures with human and literary potential. For example, Elisabeth Hauptmann, who was his frequent collaborator, provides this account of Brecht's procedure (in a conversation with me—L.B.):

> Brecht liked always to start with a proposal, a draft or something. "Write that down for me," he would say. "Bring it in black and white." He loved to change things. Perhaps his most unique quality was the astonishing way he had of seeing all the implications of what he had in mind. Suppose he thought of new dialogue. He understood at once how it would alter the meanings and relationships from beginning to end. Not one who worked with him was his equal in grasping how the small changes could alter the whole.

Perhaps commentators who presently make much of the Schweikian episodes in Brecht's life, who are endlessly fascinated by similarities of Galileo with his creator and who emphasize the passivity and masochism in Brecht's writings, might begin to give adequate emphasis to this vigorous, purposive and in her way wholly "Brechtian" figure, Vlassova.

The Mother, bristling with aggressive politics and partisan teachings, divides its audience. As the author's notes forewarn us, that is a normal and anticipated part of its function. What can the critic say of such matters that, as everyone recognizes, begin and end outside literature? Nothing, surely, that will conjure up a unanimous appraisal of this and similar works.

Readers and spectators will bring all their usual personal and political anxieties to a work so vehement as *The Mother.* Despite this, a satisfactory judgment of the aesthetic merits cannot be reached without an understanding of how the play, take it for what it is, grew organically out of Brecht's lifelong concerns. In this way the opinions against *The Mother,* prejudiced and fair, may be put into some perspective.

For one thing, the pedagogue in Brecht was always there; as his early friend Hans Otto Münsterer reports, "it always struck me even then [while *Baal* was in the writing], how much of a schoolmaster was concealed in the young revolutionary." Münsterer reports the elaborate educational schemes his friend would propose.

Take Baal, Brecht's premature hipster, hero of his first long play. Sex for Baal is engorged with that function which, later, class struggle will assume: it provides his way of relating to the world at large. Yet Baal is no self-sufficient hermit; a canny dialectician is more like it. He basks in the attentiveness of his follower Johannes. Not happy just to *be,* he would have others become so too. Johannes begs to know what is the feeling of a sexual orgasm. Baal replies: you shall learn "once you have clasped those virgin hips." Baal teaches (as the *Baden Play for Learning* subsequently will explicitly aim to teach) an "attitude." Little reliance on outright talk: the fascinating personality best engages the interest of another. Devious words, ambiguous gestures. Learning to live through your energy. Learning to live in your experience. The only worthwhile lessons are the implied result.

Baal is hardly concerned with politics. Its young author assumes, or perhaps he merely hopes, that a man may pass through the worst life offers and emerge somehow unscathed, if only his mind is lucid and his code sufficiently cynical. The "Chorale of the Great Baal" says this most clearly. *In the Jungle of Cities* has much the same outlook.

But with *A Man's A Man* Brecht no longer seems to credit the possibility of a man remaining impervious to his milieu. When Galy Gay, the porter, is reconstructed before our eyes, we see that Baal's values, his cult of independence, energy, thought, and experience have been downgraded. A message erupts that sways on the nihilist rim: personal codes, whatever their content, will succumb when the milieu (which is *man*) wants their demise enough. Thus Galy Gay's most simple wishes and needs are spotted by the British Imperial Army and their satisfaction deferred until he lets himself be rebuilt. To juxtapose the language of Marx and Stalin: His natural essence is engineered.

Yet even here, the milieu has not wholly engulfed the faculty of reason, which lives an independent existence in, not action, but *the artistic depiction*. From his rocking chair the soldier Uriah does not let us overlook it either; smoking, he directs our gaze to this and that detail of the knock-out of reason.

There is a lesson in the depiction. Yet Brecht seems bewildered to know what can be done with the capacity to reason, once its dilemma is exhibited. In this bewilderment lay his crisis as moralist and teacher.

Then, by a complex conjuncture of inner necessity and external circumstance, Brecht achieved his breakthrough to clarity. From vacation headquarters he wrote to Elisabeth Hauptmann in October, 1926: "I am eight feet deep in *Kapital*. I now must know this exactly." A year or two later, he wrote: "When I read Marx's *Kapital* I understood my plays." For Brecht, human reason had slipped into perspective.

If the proletariat as Marx said was due to terminate ownership of the means of production by individuals, thus terminating too the property system and its ideologies, then all the odious, cruel ideologies that drive the men that torment the Baals of the world and reconstruct the Galy Gays would be abolished. Obviously reason's role therefore was to assist the party of the proletariat, the Communists. With the victory of the proletariat, reason would at last come to dominate the relations men have together.

Now that Marx had given a framework to Brecht for the interpretation of his development, the least Brecht could do was help with the interpretation of Marx to the proletariat. *Lehrstücke*, the small plays for learning, were the initial outcome of Brecht's decision; they dominate his creative activity, 1929-1935. All were set to music, by Eisler, Kurt Weill, and Paul Hindemith. All centered upon social and political, philosophical and moral lessons. Most were for acting by amateurs, "learners," often children, with the audience sometimes given a part.[9] All save *The Mother* were brief. In each, the role of the reason in man's ascent was made central.

The Flight of the Lindberghs, of early 1929, recalled how man harnessed Nature to his uses only through the society-wide co-operative application of natural laws. Not one Lindbergh, but many, made the first solo trans-Atlantic flight possible. Also in 1929, the *Baden Play for Learning* quickly qualified the Lindbergh piece by indicating that man had, to date, bought ascendancy over Nature through a complementary exploitation of some classes of men by others. "Man does not help man." Taught also were the

---

9. For more about *Lehrstücke* see "Theatre for Pleasure or Theatre for Instruction," and "A Short Organum for the Theatre" in *Brecht on Theatre,* ed. John Willett, Hill & Wang: New York, 1964. See also Werner Hecht, "The Development of Brecht's Theory of Epic Theatre, 1918-1933," *Tulane Drama Review,* Sept. 1961, 40-97; and notes by Kurt Weill to *Der Jasager,* on jacket of MGM record #E3270.

consequences that face an individual who has learned the Marxist version of reason and history: he has the option of remolding his personality to become an instrument of the world-as-becoming, or of "disappearance," that is, of being doomed to inconsequentiality from the value-perspective of Marxism. *The Exception and the Rule* recapitulated the lesson of man who exploits man while exploiting Nature; added were a prologue and an epilogue that urged spectators to bring to the understanding and mastery of society the same scientific outlook that earlier had been employed to control Nature. *He Who Says Yes* and *The Measures Taken* demonstrated at an extreme pole of severity the disciplinary measures that a collectivity may impose upon adherents, when it has a social mandate and an agreed-upon task and no totally "humane" solution exists save for an irresponsible passivity that in any event would lead to worse, later.

Although not the last written, Vlassova's tale is at once the most elaborate use of the *Lehrstück* form by Brecht and the context in which lessons of the others are best comprehended. Hers is the life of one gripped by reason in history. That sense of the motion in history will not leave Brecht in his later works. It merely will not again be projected in the totality of its vision, with a central figure who so clearly thinks and behaves the way humanity, in Brecht's view, will necessarily come to think and behave. Henceforth the defeats of reasoning, partial and entire, will be shown. But always, their partial meaning will yield an implied context when examined beside *The Mother*.

Brecht also returned by 1936 to dramatic structures that were indirect and devious, "interesting" in the sense that Baal made himself "interesting" to attract receptive audiences. This major style change corresponded more or less to his loss of audiences of whatever class who could understand his own tongue, much as the onset of his *Lehrstück* period had corresponded with a decision to desert all audiences but the workers and youth. Possibly Brecht grew in leaving the *Lehrstück* form behind. But let us first understand it, in relation to his commitment and the times, as we have troubled to understand his idea development.

The German Communist vote in November, 1932 totaled nearly six million ballots. With industrial output down 40.2 percent from 1929, with but 56.2 percent of all skilled workers employed, with the overall jobless figure in excess of six million, predictions of the coming demise of capitalism might well have appeared accurate. Too, Brecht could admire the intellectual achievements of socialism in Germany. Through the years it included Marx and Engels, Lassalle, Bebel, Kautsky, Liebknecht, Luxemburg, Bernstein, Mehring, Zetkin, and scores of others of high ability and dedication. Communism seemed on the ascendant.

Nor was exposure to the revolutionary elements new to Brecht. When his native Augsburg with many other German cities set up a local Soviet in the wake of military defeat, the young Brecht was there, writing verse and taking an active if still disputed part. He did not know the theory yet; the spirit sufficed. *Drums in the Night* he first entitled *Spartakus,* the name of the Luxemburg-Liebknecht movement.

His shift in the late twenties to the left cost him severely in performances not mounted by municipal and commercial theaters. No manager took the early version of the anti-Hitler *Roundheads and Peakheads. Saint Joan of the Stockyards* was only performed over radio; no theater dared touch it.

The Mother reached the stage only through a spartan elimination of props and bulky sets together with a vigorous effort to go out to worker audiences.

The influence of curbs imposed upon his craft possibilities by *a*) the times, in view of his commitment as we have traced it, and *b*) his own strongly motivated desire to communicate with a particular audience, did much to shape the Brecht play for learning.

As examples of the second form of influence may be cited some changes Brecht made in the Gorki narrative to implement immediate political ends. Later Brecht proudly estimated that fifteen thousand German working-class women had seen this play; their image and not that of the Russian or "universal" counterpart doubtless guided Brecht in his alterations. Thus the very subject, a woman's growth into Party work, beautifully fit German Communism and Brecht weighted this aspect of the story. In May, 1931, Party head Ernst Thälmann had cited a recent Central Committee resolution as he urged more and special efforts to bring women into the organization. The tale of an extraordinary woman in this way became an example to recruit mass female adherence. In many details *The Mother* definitely promoted the Party program. Thälmann declared in 1931: "Everyone must be sent to the country with special materials, for a kind of Sunday excursion. . . . Certain villages and estates must be visited," and Vlassova does visit a country estate for purposes of making propaganda. Vigorously the Party attacked each example of working-class "opportunism," especially when it was said to come from the Social Democrats; in the play the "swamp-kopek" negotiated by conciliatory workers is turned down by Bolsheviks.

Political emphasis and shape is given even to such a complex and pervasive family concern in German society as the lack of communication between parents and children, which for a generation or two virtually all plays of integrity had mirrored, not excluding Brecht's own earlier work. Thus Vlassova and Pavel are scarcely speaking to one another at the start of *The Mother*. However, as the woman enters Party work she and her boy are bound together in the solidarity and danger of the movement. A political bridge has been thrown across the chasm. No doubt it is rickety. But Brecht may have felt this solution, as the Mother expresses it in "Praise for the Common Cause," preferable to a total lack of contact with one's elders.

The desire to project these and related political lessons might be thought compatible with a variety of dramatic forms. In the event, Brecht's choice was severely determined by hostility of the owners of conventional (and expensive) theater facilities to the intransigence he was showing. As Ernst Toller succinctly remarked: "The situation in dramatic poetry? The Reaction decides which plays appear and which do not." Nor did Brecht feel the workers and youth had much time for learning some vital matters that had better be expounded quickly. With his options thus limited he turned to the resources of Agitational Propaganda theater, dubbed "agitprop." This decision provides an essential background to *The Mother* and other *Lehrstücke,* and it may well have proved a blessing in disguise.

Brecht, with Friedrich Wolf and Gustav von Wangenheim, the other stalwarts of pro-Communist drama at this time, had to rely on agitprop techniques more or less as the alternative to writing for the desk drawer.

The established playwrights who in these years tried to tread a middle road, one that would not cost them their audience of the middle class and intellectuals, fared poorly from an artistic point of view. It is true that plays by Toller, Hasenclever, Unruh, Bruckner, Kaiser continued to be taken by the usual theaters. But nothing they wrote at the time enhanced their lifetime accomplishments. The comedies they turned out were really not funny. The thesis plays, though liberal-minded and seeking, were ravaged aesthetically by their authors' transparent confusion. Review the record of the German stage and you will find nothing in these years that matches *The Mother* or *Saint Joan of the Stockyards* in aesthetic distinction or as the expression of its time.

The agitprop influence also helped Brecht achieve a new clarity and muscular vigor in the telling of complex narratives.

Agitprop first emerged in its modern form in Russia during the years after the October Revolution, from where it spread quickly to Europe and the United States. But social or religious groups through all history have availed themselves of theater in special ways as a tool for inculcating values particularly in times of keen competition and stress. Some Jesuit efforts at anti-Communist agitprop during the thirties in St. Louis recall the roots in a past where religious emphasis predominated. The medieval morality plays mark an early stage of the agitprop tradition, and were so fostered by religious and municipal authorities. With the Calvinist Reformation young men of good family in the schools of the religious rebels and the Catholic Counter-Reformation alike acted in plays which inculcated morals, rhetoric and polity as an integral part of education.

The stunning blow of the Depression created in the late twenties and early thirties a demand for quick and firm explanation which widely disseminated the agitprop theater in Europe and America, only to have it vanish from Germany with the Nazi triumph. Its defeat elsewhere, more slow but just as certain, was accomplished by the People's Front policies. Agitprop meant vigorous caricature and denunciation of the class enemy, which could not be reconciled with wooing the middle class into a common front against Hitler. Yet in its proper epoch agitprop offered considerable advantages as political theater. It required few actors and often they could be near-amateurs. Props and scenery were packed usually in a suitcase while actors rushed by subway from one workers' hall or place of work to another, often living together in a single apartment. The cartoon-like depictions of capitalists with their lackeys, and of workers and minority peoples in their awakening and struggle, could have memorable force. Subtlety? Not desired, any more than primitive peoples strive for fine nuance in a fertility dance or a warpath rite. The reason is not due to incapacity for nuance, either. Carvings of primitives and jazz of American Negroes can provide, for example, achievements that are among man's most complexly sensitive. But for a group in struggle with pitiless

Nature or a rival people, the tendency is *to rehearse for the climactic conflict*. Imaginative seeds are sown. Pain is stoically borne in advance. Methods of triumph are anticipated. The victory is thus "assured"; while its imaginative and muscular rehearsal are both vital.

It seems apparent that the rehearsal sessions of civil-rights workers in the American South provide the current link in this theater tradition. These rehearsals in a special way parallel the requirements of a Brecht *Lehrstück*: the active, "productive" involvement of each person present is asked. Some will imitate whites and some their Negro selves while insults, beatings, even cigarette burns are inflicted. As in *The Measures Taken* and *He Who Says Yes* the discipline of adherents is tested at a pole of extreme severity. The activists of SNCC and CORE exhibit a fine sense for the learning process and the dangers ahead. The theater for learning seems not dead, but alive in places where men grow committed to an ideal and a strategy for liberating their class, their nation, their race: wherever the enemy may sharply be defined.

Brecht's own judgment of the contribution of workers' theater technique to his development may be gathered from his statement that when workers set about to act and write they prove "compellingly original."

What was known as "agitprop" art, which a number of second-rate noses were turned up at, was a treasure-lode of novel artistic techniques and means of expression. Magnificent and long-forgotten elements of truly popular art cropped up there, boldly adapted to the new social ends. Daring cuts in composition, beautiful simplifications (alongside misconceived ones); in all this there was often an astonishing economy and elegance and a fearless eye for complexity. A lot of it may have been primitive. But it was never primitive with the kind of primitivity that affected the supposedly varied psychological portrayals of bourgeois art.

The skill and discipline in discerning and imagining the "typical" that Brecht developed in these years may be thought to have contributed much to later works. This same quality provides the backbone of *The Mother*. And whatever extra-literary judgment one makes of *The Mother*, it cannot fairly be said that the work suffers for such emphasis. The German verse, though more abstract than usual, is not below its author's normal superlative standard. Agitational sorties by the Mother are dramatized with brilliance and even with much psychological nuance. And who would deny the vitality of such characters as Vlassova, the Butcher, and the teacher Vessovchikov?

The most enduring dramatic works of some authors rise directly upon agitprop foundations. One thinks of Marc Blitzstein's *The Cradle Will Rock*, Clifford Odets' *Waiting for Lefty*, and Vladimir Mayakovsky's *Bedbug*. So large a claim need not be made for *The Mother*. But it will rank high among Brecht's achievements.

—LEE BAXANDALL

THE MOTHER

CHARACTERS

The Mother, *Pelagea Vlassova*

Pavel Vlassov, *her son*

Teacher, *Nicholai Vessovchikov, brother of Ivan*

Sostakovich, *an unemployed man*

Yegor Lushin, *a striker*

Butcher, *Vassil Yefimovitch*

Butcher's Wife

Karpov, *a worker*

Smilgin, *a worker*

Anton Rybin }
André Nakhodka }
Ivan Vessovchikov } *workers*
Masha Kalatova }

Shopmistress

Policeman

Company Policeman

Commissioner

Gatekeeper

Guard

First Strikebreaker

Second Strikebreaker

Woman Worker

First Worker

Second Worker

Third Worker

First Woman

Second Woman

Third Woman

Fourth Woman

Woman in Black

Landlady

Doctor

Official

Housemaid

1

ROOM OF PELAGEA VLASSOVA

Early morning: THE MOTHER *cooks soup for her son who is going to work.*

THE MOTHER: It's such a shame to pour out soup like this for my son. Yet I can't put more fat in. Not even half a spoonful. Only last week they took a kopek an hour out of his wages and there's nothing I can do to make up for it. Don't I know he needs more nourishing food what with his long hours and heavy work. It's not easy for me to have to set such soup before my only son. He's so young, hardly grown up yet. He is so different from his father. He reads these thick books; and he never did think the food was good enough for him. And now the soup has gotten worse yet. He just gets more and more discontented.

Having poured the soup into a soup pail, she takes it over to her son. She returns to the hearth and observes as her son, not lifting his eyes from his book, removes the lid from the pail and sniffs the soup, then returns the lid and pushes the container away.

There he goes turning up his nose at the soup again. I can't do a thing to make it any better. It won't be long now, and he'll notice I am no help to him any more—just a burden. What right do I have, anyway, to eat here and live in his room and buy my clothes out of his paycheck? He'll go on his own way yet.

37

And what am I to do—I, Pelagea Vlassova, forty-two years old, the widow of a worker and the mother of a worker? Before I spend a single kopek I look and look at it. I try things first one way, then another. One time I'm skimping on wood for the fire, the next time I skimp on clothing. Nothing helps. I see nothing to be done.

Her son, PAVEL VLASSOV, *has taken his cap and the soup pail and gone.* THE MOTHER *tidies the room.*

CHORUS

Sung to The Mother by Revolutionary Workers *

Brush that skirt off
brush it again
When you're tired of brushing
you'll be left with a tidy old rag!

Cook, oh so carefully
put your best into it
If the kopeks are lacking
your soup will still be water.

Work hard; just as hard as you can,
economize, deposit your pennies
tally them ever so carefully!
If the kopeks are lacking
it won't help.

---

* The song texts here and following are not adjusted to the score composed for the play by Hanns Eisler. Excellent as that music is, those acquainted with it will know how indebted are its rhythms and phrasings to the original German text. An English that fits the Eisler music often scans awkwardly on the page. For the purposes of the present edition, therefore, the Eisler score was not taken into account.—*Trans.*

Nothing you do
will be enough.
Your spot is desperate
and getting worse.
Things can't go on this way
but what can you do?

Helpless, like the blackbird
in a winter snowstorm
that sees no way to feed its young, finds
nothing to be done, and gives way
to despair: you also see nothing you can do,
and you despair.

Nothing you do
will be enough.
Your spot is desperate
and getting worse.
Things can't go on this way
but what can you do?

You work without heed, sparing no effort
repairing the irreparable
getting what can't be gotten.
If kopeks are lacking your work is not enough.
The meat not there in your kitchen
won't get there, if you stay in your kitchen!

Nothing you do
will be enough.
Your spot is desperate
and getting worse.
Things can't go on this way
but what can you do?

2

ROOM OF PELAGEA VLASSOVA

THE MOTHER *is disturbed to see her son in the company of Revolutionary Workers.*

ANTON: Pavel, when you joined the movement two weeks ago you told us we could come here to you, when the movement had special work to be done. We have never worked here before; it's safer here with you.

PAVEL: What do you plan to do?

ANDRÉ: We need to print our leaflets for today. The working class has gotten very agitated about the new wage cuts. For three days now we have been handing out leaflets at work. Today will bring the decision. At the factory meeting this evening we will see whether we let a kopek be taken away from us, or we strike!

IVAN: We brought along the hectograph and paper.

PAVEL: Please, sit down. My mother will make tea.

They go to the table.

ANTON: Where is Sidor?

MASHA: My brother didn't come. Going home last night, he saw someone following him who seemed to be a policeman. So he decided to go straight to the factory today.

PAVEL: Talk quietly. It is better if my mother doesn't hear us. I have never told her anything about these things. She's no longer young. And she couldn't be of use in any case.

ANTON: Here's the stencil.

They begin working. A heavy cloth has been hung over the window.

THE MOTHER (*aside*): I don't like to see my son Pavel get mixed up with this kind of people. Before it ends they'll have led him away from me. They make him excited and involve him in the Lord knows what. I don't set out tea for such people. (*She goes to the table.*) Pavel, I'm afraid I can't boil any tea. We haven't enough. With what there is I couldn't make decent tea.

PAVEL: Then make some thin tea for us, mother.

THE MOTHER (*has gone back and seated herself on a chair*): Now if I don't do it, they'll be sure to see that I don't care for them. Just what right do they have to come in here and talk so softly I can't hear a thing! (*She goes back to the table.*) Pavel, I don't want to have the landlord noticing how people come here at five in the morning to print things. That won't help in the least to pay our rent.

IVAN: Mrs. Vlassova, you must believe us. We are more interested in your rent than in anything else. As a matter of fact, that is all we really care about; although it may not look that way.

THE MOTHER: I just don't know about that. (*She goes back.*)

ANTON: Pavel, your mother's not pleased to have us here, is she?

IVAN: She finds it very difficult to understand that we must do this here just so she can buy tea and pay her rent.

THE MOTHER: Well they surely have thick skins! It's as though they noticed nothing at all. What are their plans with Pavel? He was glad to have the job, when he first went to work. It's true he wasn't paid much. And in the past year its gotten smaller and smaller. If they take still another kopek away from him, I'd rather not eat myself. But it's disturbing to see the way he reads all those books; and I worry about the way he and this crowd run around together and he gets all excited instead of getting his sleep at night. This way, he'll only lose his job.

MASHA (*sings to* THE MOTHER):

THE SONG OF WHAT TO DO

If you have an empty plate
how do you expect to sup?
It's up to you to take the state
and turn it over, bottoms up,
till you have filled your plate.
Help yourself—no need to wait!

If there's no work and you're a poor man
how do you intend to sup?
It's up to you to take the state
and turn it over, bottoms up,
till you yourself become the foreman.
Then there'll be work, there'll be no poor man!

Do they laugh and call you weak?
Don't waste time—start your promotion!

Bring the plan for action to the meek,
See that they have got in motion.
Soon their time will come to speak.
Laughter then will ring among the weak.

VOICES FROM OUTSIDE: Be careful—the police are coming!

ANDRÉ: Hide the paper!

IVAN *closes the door.* ANDRÉ, *taking the hectograph from Pavel's hands, hangs it outside the window.* ANTON *seats himself upon the paper.*

THE MOTHER: Pavel, listen! the police are here now. Pavel, what are you mixed up in; what do those papers say?

MASHA (*leads her to the window and seats her in a chair*): Please, Mrs. Vlassova, just sit here quietly.

IVAN *opens the door. A* POLICEMAN *and a* COMMISSIONER *enter.*

POLICEMAN: Halt! Anyone who moves, I'll shoot! There's his mother, sir. And there he himself is!

COMMISSIONER: I am here to search your house, Pavel Vlassov. Ah, but what kind of a lousy bunch is this to be mixed up with?

POLICEMAN: This one here is the sister of Sidor Kalatov who we arrested early today. These are the right ones, all right.

MASHA: What have you done with my brother?

COMMISSIONER: Your brother conveys his best wishes; we have him. Momentarily he preaches revolution to the bedbugs and is enjoying a large congregation. Sadly enough, he doesn't have any leaflets.

The Workers glance at each other.

COMMISSIONER: As I recall, we still have one or two adjacent cells vacant. Didn't I hear the lilt of a beautiful song being sung just now? Oh, I beg you, do not let my presence prevent you; I too am musical. I only regret, my dear Mrs. Vlassova, that it was in your house that this particular song had to be sung—for now I have to look around and see if I can locate the score. We of the police would like to be able to sing along too, even if our voices are perhaps a little harsh. (*He goes to the divan.*) Please notice, Vlassova; for example, I am forced now to tear open your divan. Is this what you wanted?

PAVEL: You don't find any rubles in there, do you? That's because we are workers and do not earn very much.

COMMISSIONER: And what of this mirror upon your wall? Must it be shattered by the cruel hand of the policeman? (*He smashes it.*) You are a respectable woman, as I am aware. And it is true, there was nothing in the divan which might be considered unrespectable. But what of this fine old chest of drawers? (*He overturns it.*) Well, just look; nothing here either! Vlassova, Vlassova! Decent people are not sly. Ought you to be sly? Then here is the lardpot with its little spoon; the old, sentimental lardpot. (*Lifts it from the whatnot, lets it drop.*) Ah, now it has fallen onto the floor —now we can all see there is only lard inside.

PAVEL: Not much. There isn't much lard in it, Commissioner. In the breadbox there isn't much bread, either; and in the jar there isn't much tea.

COMMISSIONER (*to the* POLICEMAN): In that case I believe it must be a political lardpot. Vlassova, Vlassova, why must you tangle with us bloodhounds in your old age? Your curtains are kept so clean. One scarcely ever sees the like. It's a genuine treat to see them. (*He rips them down.*)

IVAN (*to* ANTON, *who, fearing for the hectograph, has leaped up*): Sit down! You'll be shot.

PAVEL (*loudly, diverting the* COMMISSIONER): Why did you have to throw the lardpot on the floor?

ANDRÉ (*to the* POLICEMAN): Pick up the lardpot!

POLICEMAN: This one's André Nakhodka, he's from Little Russia.

COMMISSIONER (*walks to the table*): André Maximovitch Nakhodka—isn't it true that you have more than once been thrown into jail for offenses of a political nature?

ANDRÉ: Yes. In Rostov, and in Saratov. But the police there had some manners.

COMMISSIONER (*pulls a leaflet from his pocket*): Well, *sir*. Might you possibly know which are the rascals who circulate this very treasonous leaflet within the factory?

PAVEL: We've just now set eyes on our first rascals.

COMMISSIONER: You, Pavel Vlassov, you are going to learn your place. Sit respectfully when I speak to you!

THE MOTHER: You must not shout so! Please, you are a young man still, and you never had to suffer. You're an official. They pay you a lot of money, regularly, so you can come in here and cut open our divan and see there is no lard in our lardpot.

COMMISSIONER: You cry too soon, Vlassova. I advise you to save your tears; you will need them. Rather pay more attention to your son. He's on the wrong path. (*To the Workers:*) The day will come when your slyness will do you no more good. (*He exits.*)

IVAN (*listening at the door*): They've gone.

The Workers clean up.

ANTON: We must beg your forgiveness, Pelagea Vlassova. We had no idea they suspected us already. Now your home has been wrecked.

MASHA: Are you very much frightened, Mrs. Vlassova?

THE MOTHER: Yes. I can see that Pavel is on the wrong path.

MASHA: Well, but do you think it is right that your home is wrecked just because your son fights for his kopeks?

THE MOTHER: They do not do the right thing. But he isn't doing the right thing, either.

IVAN (*at the table again*): How are the leaflets going to get distributed?

ANTON: Supposing we don't hand out leaflets today, just because the police are beginning to catch on. Then we'll have been nothing but windbags. The leaflets have to be handed out.

ANDRÉ: How many of them?

PAVEL: About five hundred.

IVAN: Who will hand them out?

ANTON: It's the turn of Pavel today.

THE MOTHER *beckons* IVAN *over to her.*

THE MOTHER: Who is supposed to hand out leaflets?

IVAN: Pavel. But it's not so dangerous.

THE MOTHER: It's not dangerous! You want to send Pavel and you tell him it's not dangerous.

IVAN: It's necessary.

THE MOTHER: It's necessary! The reading of books and coming home late is what begins it. Then there's working here in the house, with machines that have to be hung outside the window. In front of the window there has to be a curtain hung. And everything is carried on in soft voices. It's necessary! Then, suddenly, things don't go right any more at the factory. I hear nothing about all this. The next thing is the police walk into my house and act like a person were a criminal. (*She rises.*) I demand that you turn down this job, Pavel.

ANDRÉ: Mrs. Vlassova, it is necessary.

PAVEL (*to* MASHA): Tell her the leaflets have to be handed out on account of Sidor; so he will be let free.

The Workers go over to THE MOTHER. PAVEL *remains seated at the table.*

MASHA: It is also necessary, Mrs. Vlassova, on account of my brother.

IVAN: Or else Sidor can expect Siberia.

ANDRÉ: Don't you see: if no more leaflets are handed out today, they'll know it must have been Sidor who handed them out yesterday.

MASHA: Certainly. Even fools will notice that. Yesterday leaflets were smuggled into the factory. They arrest a man, and today the smuggling stops. It's clear that the man they arrested did it.

ANTON: That's why it's necessary for the leaflets to be handed out again today.

THE MOTHER: It's necessary, I see that. It's true something must be done to rescue this young man you have dragged into things from being destroyed. But what will they do to Pavel if he's arrested?

ANTON: It's not so dangerous.

THE MOTHER: So it's not so dangerous. A man has been led astray and drawn in. If he's to be saved, this and that is necessary. It is not dangerous, but it is necessary. Although we're suspected, we have to hand out leaflets. It is necessary; that's why it's not dangerous. That's how it goes. Finally, a man stands upon the gallows. Just slip your head into the noose, it's not dangerous. Let me have the leaflets. I, not Pavel, will go and hand them out.

ANTON: But how do you plan it?

IVAN: Nobody must know who gives the leaflets out.

THE MOTHER: Don't you worry about that. I can do it as well as ever you could. During the noon lunch break, my friend Maria Korsunova sells lunches at the factory. Today, I will take her place. I'll wrap the food in your leaflets. (*She goes to get her shopping bag.*)

MASHA: Pavel, your mother has asked if she can distribute the leaflets. It speaks well of her.

PAVEL: It's up to you to weigh the advantages for or against. Please, I ask you, don't make me decide on my mother's offer.

ANTON: André?

ANDRÉ: I think she can do it. She is known by the workers, and the police aren't suspicious of her.

ANTON: Ivan?

IVAN: I think she can too.

ANTON: Supposing she is caught, less can happen to her than to us. She isn't in the movement, so, obviously, she's done it for her son. Comrade Vlassov: in view of the dangerous situation and the grave threat to our comrade, we wish to accept your mother's offer.

IVAN: We believe she will run the least danger.

PAVEL: It's all right with me.

THE MOTHER (*to herself*): I am sure this is a very bad cause I'm about to help—but I must keep Pavel out of it.

ANTON: We are entrusting this packet of leaflets to you, Mrs. Vlassova.

ANDRÉ: So, now you will be fighting for us, Pelagea Vlassova, won't you?

THE MOTHER: Fighting? I am hardly a young woman and
I am not a fighter. If I can manage to scrape together
my three kopeks, I'm happy. There is fight enough
for me.

ANDRÉ: You don't know what the leaflets say, Mrs. Vlassova?

THE MOTHER: No. I'm not able to read.

3

SUKLINOV WORKS:
THE FACTORY YARD

THE MOTHER *hands out leaflets during the noon hour at the Suklinov Works.*

THE MOTHER (*with a big basket, at the factory gate*): It all depends upon what kind of a man this gatekeeper is. Whether he's a lazy or a careful one. What I have to do is to get a pass out of him. What I'll do next is wrap the food in the leaflets. So then if they catch me, I'll simply say someone must have smuggled them into my basket, since I can't read. (*She studies the* GATEKEEPER.) He looks to be a fat and lazy fellow. We'll just see what happens when I hold a pickle out to him! It's this kind that love to stuff themselves and they never have anything. (*Going to the gate, she lets drop a parcel in front of the* GATEKEEPER.) You, if you please, I've dropped a package.

The GATEKEEPER *looks the other way.*

Now isn't that strange! I completely forgot I only have to put down my basket to have my hands free. And there I almost went and troubled you. (*To the audienc*e:) He's a hard-boiled type. But if you gossip away at them they'll do anything, just to get some peace and quiet. (*She goes to the entrance and speaks rapidly.*) Now wouldn't you just expect that of Maria Korsunova! No more than the day before yesterday

I said to her: Do anything you like, but don't get wet feet! Do you think she listened to me? No. Out she went to dig potatoes, and she got wet feet again. Then the very next morning she goes to feed her goats. Wet feet! What do you think of that? With all of this it wasn't long before she was flat on her back, of course. But instead of resting in bed, she goes out again at night. Naturally, it rained, and what do you imagine she got? Wet feet!

GATEKEEPER: You cannot enter without a pass.

THE MOTHER: Isn't that just what I told her! But it does no good. Wet feet! Even so, I'm her best friend. We are one heart and one soul, you know, but never in your life did you see such stubbornness! I'm sick, Vlassova, I want you to go to the factory in my place and sell the food. Look here, Maria, I say, you are hoarse now—but tell me why you are hoarse? And she says: if you are going to still go on nagging me about those wet feet, and if all you can think of is to blame me, then I am going to crack this cup over your thick head! Such a stubborn one!

GATEKEEPER (*sighing, lets her pass*): On your way!

THE MOTHER: You're perfectly right. All I'm doing is keeping you.

It is the noon lunch break. Workers sit on boxes, etc., eating. THE MOTHER *vends her victuals.* IVAN *helps her wrap them.*

THE MOTHER: Pickles, tobacco, tea, meat pies!

IVAN: And they're wrapped in the best of paper.

THE MOTHER: Pickles, tobacco, tea, meat pies!

IVAN: And no charge for the paper they're wrapped in.

FIRST WORKER: Do you have any pickles?

THE MOTHER: Yes, here are pickles.

IVAN: And don't throw away the paper they're wrapped in.

THE MOTHER: Pickles, tobacco, tea, meat pies.

SECOND WORKER: Can you tell me what's written on the paper that's so interesting? I can't read.

THIRD WORKER: How do I know what's there on your paper?

FIRST WORKER: I'll tell you, buddy—the same thing's there in *your* fist!

SECOND WORKER: That's right. There *is* something here.

FIRST WORKER: Well?

SECOND WORKER: They're perfectly right. Once we start to bargain, we're done for.

THE MOTHER (*to all the yard*): Pickles, tobacco, tea, meat pies.

THIRD WORKER: The police are hot after them already. The factory security has been tightened too. But here's a new leaflet they've gotten out. They are a clever bunch of fellows; nothing will stop them. Yes, and there's a lot of truth to what they say.

FIRST WORKER: What I say is, when I see a thing like this, I'm for it.

KARPOV: Are all the people we can trust here?

The trustworthy Workers of the company all gather in a corner of the factory yard. Among them are ANTON *and* PAVEL.

KARPOV: We have been bargaining, brothers!

ANTON: What did you get?

KARPOV: It is not with empty hands, brothers, that we come back to you.

ANTON: Did you get the kopek?

KARPOV: We tallied it up for Mr. Suklinov, brothers; and we showed him that it comes to twenty-four thousand rubles a year, when he takes a kopek an hour out of the wages of eight hundred workers. The twenty-four thousand rubles were supposed to go into the pocket of Mr. Suklinov. We had to stop him no matter what! Well—following a four hour struggle, we got what we wanted. We stopped him. Those twenty-four thousand rubles are not going into the pocket of Mr. Suklinov.

ANTON: Did you get the kopek back, then?

KARPOV: We have always insisted, brothers, that the plant's sanitary conditions are intolerable.

PAVEL: Did you get that kopek?

KARPOV: Just before our factory's east gate lie swamps which are a profound evil.

ANTON: So that's it! He plans to use it on the swamp.

KARPOV: Bear in mind the clouds of gnats which come every summer, making it impossible for us to go out in the open air. Remember how many become sick from swamp fever; remember the constant threat to our children. The swamp can be drained, brothers, for twenty-four thousand rubles. Mr. Suklinov is prepared to undertake it. An expansion of the factory has been planned for the lands which would be reclaimed. New jobs would emerge from this. What is good for the factory, as you know, is also good for you. Brothers: the company is doing less well than we perhaps believe. A bit of information has been passed on to us by Mr. Suklinov, which we cannot withhold from you; the Tver factory competing with ours is being closed down. Starting tomorrow, seven hundred of our brothers will be out on the street. We believe in the lesser evil. We are presently upon the threshhold of one of the greatest economic crises ever experienced by our nation—as every clear-sighted man sees with alarm.

PAVEL: What you mean is, capitalism is ailing and you are the doctor. Do you mean to say you're for taking the wage cut?

KARPOV: No other solution has emerged from our bargaining.

ANTON: Since you are unable to stop the wage cut, we demand that you stop negotiations with management. The swamp kopek is rejected.

KARPOV: I warn against breaking off the bargaining.

FIRST WORKER: Can't you see this means a strike?

PAVEL: We think only a strike can save the kopek.

ANTON: The meeting today has a very simple question to answer: should the kopek be saved or should Mr. Suklinov's swamp be drained? There's no way to avoid the strike. And by the First of May, which gives us only a week, we must get other plants where wages are being cut to close down!

PAVEL and he leave.

KARPOV: Do you think I should go on bargaining, considering the circumstances?

SECOND WORKER: Everybody in the factory yard reads their leaflets, Karpov, in spite of the police security. These types are very sly; I'm afraid we don't have our people in hand any longer. There isn't much appeal left in draining the swamp. That slogan about the "swamp kopek" will finish us.

The whistle blows, and the others go back into the factory now.

KARPOV (*left alone*): Well, so strike!

GATEKEEPER (*finds a leaflet on the ground*): What's this here? Another one of those inflammatory leaflets? (*He telephones.*) Jefim, Company Police!

THE MOTHER (*coming forward*): Pickles, tobacco, tea, meat pies.

KARPOV: A pickle.

THE MOTHER sells him a pickle. She sits down to count her proceeds.

THE MOTHER: (*to herself*): A reduction in the pay would be bad. It is a great wrong, and to me especially— because if the wages go down and down, how shall I make out with Pavel? He is so discontented already.

KARPOV (*comes over to her*): Is it you who hands these out, then? Do you understand that this little piece of paper means a strike?

THE MOTHER: A strike? Why is that?

KARPOV: These leaflets summon the employees of the Suklinov Works to strike.

THE MOTHER: I know nothing about it.

KARPOV: Then why do you hand them out?

THE MOTHER: We have our reasons. Why do they arrest our people?

KARPOV: You mean you don't even know what it says here?

THE MOTHER: No. I'm not able to read.

KARPOV: That's how these people stir us up. A strike is a bad thing. Tomorrow morning they won't go back to work. What will it be like, tomorrow night? And next week, how will matters stand? It doesn't matter to the company whether we ever work again. To us it is life itself.

The COMPANY POLICEMAN *comes on the run.*

COMPANY POLICEMAN: What's the trouble?

The GATEKEEPER *shows the leaflet to him.*

I just picked up two of these myself.

GATEKEEPER: And here's another.

POLICEMAN (*to* KARPOV): What's that you're reading? (*He seizes him.*) Where did you get that leaflet?

THE MOTHER: But this man is innocent! I am positive he didn't hand out leaflets.

KARPOV: Let go. You let me go!

POLICEMAN (*strikes him*): Take this for you and your leaflets!

THE MOTHER: But all the man did was buy a pickle.

4

ROOM OF PELAGEA VLASSOVA

The comrades are reproached by THE MOTHER, *because of the results of distributing the leaflets. She gets her first lesson in Communism.*

THE MOTHER: Pavel, I distributed the leaflets today that you all gave me, just as you asked me to. I did it so they won't suspect that young man you brought into this. But when I was finished handing them out, before my own eyes I saw three more people arrested, and the only thing they did was read the leaflets. What have you done with me?

ANTON: We thank you, Mrs. Vlassova, for your clever work.

THE MOTHER: Do you call that cleverness? And what about Karpov who is in prison, because I am so clever?

ANDRÉ: It wasn't you who put him in prison. The way we see it, the police put him in prison.

IVAN: While you had a part in uniting the workers of the Suklinov Works. I guess you heard the strike was voted; almost unanimously.

THE MOTHER: I had no wish to make a strike. I just wanted to help a human being. Far from helping, I have gotten three others arrested. Why Sidor? Why those three others? Why were they arrested? Just because they read leaflets? Why are you striking? What does the leaflet say?

ANTON: It was good work in a good cause, when you handed it out.

THE MOTHER: What does the leaflet say?

PAVEL: What do you think it said?

THE MOTHER: Something very wrong.

ANTON: Mrs. Vlassova, we can see we owe you an explanation.

PAVEL: Sit down with us, mother. We want to explain it to you.

They get chairs, and seat themselves around THE MOTHER.

IVAN: Well, you see; the leaflet says the workers should not put up with it when Mr. Suklinov cuts the wages just as he pleases.

THE MOTHER: Nonsense. What do you hope to do about it? Why don't you think Mr. Suklinov should cut the wages he pays you just as he pleases? Is it or isn't it his factory?

PAVEL: It does belong to him.

THE MOTHER: You see, then. This table belongs to me, for instance. Now let me ask you whether I can't do just as I want with this table?

ANDRÉ: Sure, Mrs. Vlassova. You can do just what you want with this table.

THE MOTHER: You see. Can I chop it up for kindling wood
if I want?

ANTON: Yes. You can make kindling wood out of your
table.

THE MOTHER: Well? If that's so, then can't Mr. Suklinov
do what he wants with his factory—since it belongs
to him just like my table belongs to me?

PAVEL: No.

THE MOTHER: Why do you say no?

IVAN: It's because he needs workers in his factory.

THE MOTHER: But what happens when he says he doesn't
need you any longer?

PAVEL: Mother, look here, you must think of it this way.
Sometimes he has need of using us and sometimes he
doesn't.

ANTON: That's right.

PAVEL: When he needs us we must be there. When
he doesn't need us, we are there anyway. Where
could we go? And he understands this. He doesn't
always need us, but we always need him. He counts
on this. Although those are Mr. Suklinov's machines,
they are also our tools. We have no others. We have
no weaving looms, and we have no lathes, for the
very reason that we make use of Mr. Suklinov's
machines. His factory is his property. But when he
closes it he takes away our tools.

THE MOTHER: That's because your tools belong to him,
just the way my table belongs to me.

ANTON: Yes; but do you think it is right for our tools to belong to him?

THE MOTHER (*loudly*): No I do not! But they still belong to him, whether I think it is right or wrong. Maybe someone else doesn't think it's right that my table belongs to me.

PAVEL: Well, listen; to that we say: there is a big difference between whether a table or a factory belongs to you. A table really can belong to you. So can a chair. Nobody is hurt by it. Suppose you feel like setting them up on your roof; what harm can it do? But when a factory belongs to you, you can hurt hundreds of men with it. In this case, you are a man who owns *others'* tools; and you can use them to get use out of men.

THE MOTHER: Well, of course he can use us. Don't you suppose I have noticed that over the space of thirty years? But there is one thing I have not noticed; which is that anyone is able to do anything about it.

ANTON: Getting back to Mr. Suklinov's property, Pelagea Vlassova; we were to the point where his factory is a different kind of property than, for example, your table. He can use his property to use us.

IVAN: There's another unusual thing about his property. Unless he is using us with it, it's no good at all to him. It's only worth something to him so long as it is our tool. The moment it stops being our means of production, it turns into a bare heap of scrap iron. Even with all his property, you see, he cannot get along without us.

THE MOTHER: Fine. But how do you think you'll prove to him that he needs you?

ANDRÉ: It's like this. Suppose this fellow, Pavel Vlassov, walks up to Mr. Suklinov and he says, Mr. Suklinov, without me your factory is nothing but a bare heap of scrap iron and that's why you cannot cut my wages just as you please. Well, Mr. Suklinov just laughs and throws out this fellow Vlassov. But if every Vlassov in Tver—eight hundred Vlassovs—get up and say the same thing, Mr. Suklinov will have to stop laughing.

THE MOTHER: And that's what your strike is?

PAVEL: Right. That is our strike.

THE MOTHER: And that is what's in the leaflet?

PAVEL: Yes. That is what's in the leaflet.

THE MOTHER: A strike like that is a bad thing. What do you expect me to cook? Where will the rent come from? Tomorrow morning you won't go to work. How will things stand tomorrow night? And what will matters be next week? Well and good; we will get through all that, somehow. But if the only thing in here is about the strike, why are people arrested by the police? Why does it concern the police?

PAVEL: Yes, mother. We ask you that: why does it concern the police?

THE MOTHER: If we make a strike against Mr. Suklinov, that's no concern of the police, is it? Maybe you have gotten it wrong. There must be a mistake. Everybody thinks you will want to do something violent. What you ought to do is show all the city that your quarrel with the management is decent and peaceful. That way, you'll make a big impression.

IVAN: Mrs. Vlassova, that is exactly what we plan to do. On the First of May, the international day of the workers' struggle, every factory in Tver will be demonstrating for the liberation of the working class. We are going to carry posters asking each factory in Tver to support our fight for the kopek.

THE MOTHER: If you march quietly through the streets and just carry posters, nobody can have a thing against it.

ANDRÉ: We expect that Mr. Suklinov will not want to go along with it.

THE MOTHER: Well, he must go along with it.

IVAN: Probably the police will break up the demonstration.

THE MOTHER: What do the police and Mr. Suklinov have to do with each other? The police are over you, it's true; but they're just as much over Mr. Suklinov.

PAVEL: Mother, I guess you think the police won't do anything against a peaceful demonstration?

THE MOTHER: Yes, that is what I think. Since there's no violence in it. Never could we agree on anything violent, Pavel. I believe, as you know, in a God in Heaven. I'll have nothing to do with violence. Although I have known nothing else for forty years, I could never do anything against it. But I hope at least that, when I die, I'll have done nothing violent.

5

A STREET

The First of May. The Workers of Tver demonstrate against the wage cut.

PAVEL: We workers of the Suklinov Works were just crossing the wool market, when we came upon a column from the other plants. Already there were many thousands of us. We carried posters that declared: Workers, support our fight against the wage cut! Join our fight!

IVAN: We marched quietly in good order. Some songs were sung: Arise, Ye Prisoners of Starvation, and Comrades, the Bugles Are Sounding. Our factory came along right behind the great red flag.

ANDRÉ: Next to me, close behind her son, marched Pelagea Vlassova. When we came for him early in the morning, she suddenly came out of the kitchen fully dressed, and when we asked where she was going, she said to us:

THE MOTHER: I'm going with you.

ANTON: Many like her were with us; for many had come over to us, because of the hard winter, the wage cuts in the factories, and our agitation. We saw a few policemen and no soldiers at all, before we came to the Boulevard of Our Savior. But at the corner of the Boulevard of Our Savior and the Tverskaya, a double line of policemen suddenly was standing there. They spotted our flags and our posters and a voice suddenly called out to us: Attention! Halt and disperse, or we will shoot! Also: Drop the flag! Our column came to a halt.

PAVEL: But since marchers at the rear were still moving forward, those who were in front could not stand their ground, and then there was shooting. Although the first in line milled back, what happened was confusion. Many there could not believe that what they saw had really happened. At this point the police began to move upon the crowd.

THE MOTHER: I went along to help demonstrate for the workers' cause. The people marching there were decent, orderly people, who had worked hard all their lives. There were also, of course, some desperate people, driven to extremes because they had no jobs; also some hungry people, too weak to defend themselves.

ANDRÉ: Since we were standing well to the front, when the shooting began we did not disperse.

PAVEL: We had our flag still. Smilgin was carrying it; and we had no thought of giving it up for now it seemed to us, although we did not understand how, that they felt it was important to stop us, knock us down, and take our flag, the red flag, yes ours, to take it way. But what we wanted was for all the workers to see who we are and what we are for; which is for the workers!

ANDRÉ: The men against us were driven to act like wild animals. Why else did the Suklinovs pay them their living?

MASHA: Everybody would come to see it in the end, and this flag, our red one, had to be held especially high and in the sight of all—the policemen, of course, but in sight of all the others too.

IVAN: As for those who were not there to see it, they would be told about it, if not today then tomorrow, or in the years to come, until such a time as it was seen again. For our own part we knew very well, and many at this moment were sure of it: it would be seen again, and again, from now on, until everything in our line of march was completely changed. Our flag, the most threatening of all to exploiters and rulers. And unstoppable!

ANTON: And for the workers, the supreme flag!

ALL: And so you will see it
again and again
gladly or ungladly
according to your place in this struggle
which cannot end otherwise
than with our total victory
in all the cities of all countries
where there are workers.

THE MOTHER: But on this particular day, it was carried by the worker Smilgin.

SMILGIN: For fifteen years I have been in the movement. I was one of the first to carry the revolutionary message in the factory. We have fought for better pay and better working conditions. I often have bargained with the owners in this cause, and in the interests of my brothers. I hated to, at first; but after a time, I must admit, I thought it the easier way. If, I thought, we were to increase our power, we must reconcile ourselves to bargaining. That was all wrong. I stand here now, and many thousands already at my back; and before us, once again, it is Power that confronts us. Do we give up the flag?

ANTON: Don't give it up, Smilgin! You cannot bargain with them, we said; and the Mother said to him:

THE MOTHER: You must not give it up. Nothing can happen to you. The police won't do anything against a peaceful demonstration.

MASHA: At this moment a police officer called out to us: Hand over the flag!

IVAN: And Smilgin looked back and saw, behind his flag, our posters; and on the posters, our demands. And those were strikers from the Suklinov Works who stood behind the posters. We watched to see what would be done with the flag by this man who stood next to us, one of us.

PAVEL: Fifteen years in the movement; worker; revolutionary; on the First of May, 1905, 11 o'clock in the morning, at the corner of the Boulevard of Our Savior; the decisive moment. He said:

SMILGIN: I won't give it up! We are not bargaining.

ANDRÉ: Good, Smilgin, we said. That's the way. Now everything will be all right.

IVAN: Yes, he said, and he fell forward upon his face, for they had shot him.

ANDRÉ: And they ran toward him, four or five men, to seize the flag. The flag lay beside him. At that moment our Pelagea Vlassova, Vlassova the quiet one, the even-tempered, our comrade, bent down and reached for the flag.

THE MOTHER: Let me have the flag, Smilgin, I said. Give it here! I will take it. All of this must be changed!

6

HOME OF THE
TEACHER VESSOVCHIKOV

Following the arrest of PAVEL, IVAN *takes* THE MOTHER
to his brother Nicholai, a TEACHER.

IVAN: I bring you, Nicholai Ivanovitch, Pelagea Vlassova
—the mother of our friend Pavel. Her son was arrested because of the First of May demonstration.
They gave her notice to get out of her old home;
so we made a promise to her son to look after her.
You and your house are not suspected. There isn't
a soul who would dream of saying you've had anything to do with the revolutionary movement.

TEACHER: Certainly not; you are telling the truth. As a
teacher, I would be fired from my position, were I
to chase after such chimeras as you do.

IVAN: I hope, in any case, you will keep Mrs. Vlassova
here with you. She has nowhere else to go. As my
brother you will be doing me a great favor.

TEACHER: I see no reason why I should do you a favor.
I disapprove of your activities, all of them, completely. They amount to utter nonsense. I have proven
this often enough to you. But these are not matters
which touch you, Mrs. Vlassova. Your plight is
apparent. I have, moreover, been somewhat in need

71

of a person to look after this place. As you can see, it is in disorder.

IVAN: You have to pay her something for her work, of course. Once in a while she has to send something to her son.

TEACHER: You must understand I can pay only a very small allowance.

IVAN: He understands politics about as well as does this chair. But he's not inhuman.

TEACHER: Ivan, you are a fool. The kitchen is here, Mrs. Vlassova. There is a sofa where you may sleep, in the kitchen. I see you brought along your linens. Here is the kitchen, Mrs. Vlassova.

THE MOTHER *goes into the kitchen with her bundle, and starts organizing herself there.*

IVAN: I want personally to thank you, Nicholai Ivanovitch! And, please, take care of the woman. She should have nothing further to do with politics. Now she has been involved in the First of May disturbance, she should have her peace. She worries about what will happen to her son. I hold you responsible for her.

TEACHER: Have no worry, I will not draw her into politics—that is what you people do.

THE TEACHER VESSOVCHIKOV
SURPRISES VLASSOVA AT HER PROPAGANDA WORK

Workers are seated around THE MOTHER, *in the kitchen.*

WOMAN: They tell us that Communism is a crime.

THE MOTHER: That is simply not true. Communism is good for us. What is this talk against Communism? (*She sings.*)

PRAISE OF COMMUNISM

It's sensible, anyone can understand it. It's easy.
If you're not an exploiter, you can grasp it.
It's good for you; find out about it.
The stupid call it stupid, and the rotten call it rotten
it's against what's rotten, and against stupidity.
The exploiters call it a crime.
But we know
it is the end of crime.
It is not madness,
but the end of madness.
It is not chaos
but order.
It is the simple thing
so hard to bring about.

WOMAN: If that is so, why don't all the workers see it?

SOSTAKOVICH: Because they are kept in ignorance of being exploited, and of knowing this is a crime and that it is possible to put an end to the crime.

As the TEACHER *enters the adjacent room they cease talking.*

TEACHER: I come home tired from the tavern, my head still buzzing from the aggravating arguments of that idiot Sakkar, who always contradicts me though I am certainly in the right—and I at once feel at peace within my own four walls. I believe I will have a footbath, and read my newspaper.

THE MOTHER: (*entering*): Oh, are you home already, Nicholai Ivanovitch?

TEACHER: I am. May I ask you to prepare me a hot footbath? I will take it in the kitchen.

THE MOTHER: I am so glad you have come home, Nicholai Ivanovitch. So glad, because now you must go out again. As the woman next door was just telling me, your friend Sakkar Smerdyakov was here just about an hour ago. He has to talk with you, and he could not leave a message because he must speak with you at once, and personally! You must quickly go look for him! Go on, now, quickly! What with your inborn liking for comfort, you have more than once neglected your duties. Besides, you should be glad to do a personal favor for Mr. Smerdyakov. As I said, he was here, less than an hour ago.

TEACHER: Pelagea Vlassova, I spent the entire evening with my friend Sakkar Smerdyakov.

THE MOTHER: Ah? But the kitchen is such a mess, Nicholai Ivanovitch. I've hung the washing up.

Whispering in the kitchen.

TEACHER: Since when does my washing engage in gossip while it dries, and (*pointing at the samovar in her hands*) how long have my shirts been drinking tea?

THE MOTHER: Nicholai Ivanovitch, I must confess; we are sitting around talking, over a cup of tea.

TEACHER: So. And what sort of people are these?

THE MOTHER: I do not know whether you would feel

comfortable with them, Nicholai Ivanovitch. These are not well-to-do people.

TEACHER: Aha. Then you are talking politics again! Is that unemployed fellow, Sostakovich, among them?

THE MOTHER: Yes; and his wife, and his brother, and his brother's son, and his aunt and uncle. They are all very bright people, and I know you would follow their discussion with interest.

TEACHER: Pelagea Vlassova, have I not made it perfectly clear to you that I wish no politics in my household? Here I return home tired from my tavern, only to find my kitchen full of politics. I am astonished, Mrs. Vlassova; astonished.

THE MOTHER: Nicholai Ivanovitch, I am so sorry I had to disappoint you. I was just telling the people about the First of May. They don't know enough about it.

TEACHER: What do you know of politics, Mrs. Vlassova? Only tonight I was telling my friend Sakkar, who is, by the way, a very intelligent man: "Sakkar Smerdya-kov, nothing on earth is more difficult and hard to understand than politics."

THE MOTHER: I know how tired and tense you must be. Yet, if you had just a little time—all of us were agreed tonight, that you could explain a lot to us about things that are hard to understand; about the First of May too.

TEACHER: I suppose you know how little I desire to get in a quarrel with that unemployed fellow, Sostako-vich. At the very most, I might attempt to supply a few of the fundamentals of politics. Bring along the samovar; and some bread, and maybe a few pickles.

They take these into the kitchen.

THE MOTHER LEARNS TO READ

TEACHER (*before a blackboard*): All right, you want to learn to read. I cannot understand why you need it, in your situation; you are also rather old. But I will try, just as a favor for Mrs. Vlassova. Have you all something to write with? All right then, I will now write three easy words here: "Branch, nest, fish." I repeat: "Branch, nest, fish." (*He writes.*)

THE MOTHER (*who sits at the table with three others*): Must it really be "Branch, nest, fish"? Because we are old people we have to learn the words we need quickly!

TEACHER (*smiles*): I beg your pardon; but the reason you may have for learning to read is a matter of total indifference.

THE MOTHER: Why should it be? Tell me, for instance, how do you write the word "Worker"? That will be of interest to our Pavel Sostakovich.

SOSTAKOVICH: Who needs to know how to write "Branch"?

THE MOTHER: He is a metal worker.

TEACHER: But you will need the letters in the word.

WORKER: But the letters in the words "Class Struggle" are needed too!

TEACHER: Possibly; but we must begin with the simplest things and not at once with the hardest! "Branch" is simple.

SOSTAKOVICH: "Class Struggle" is much more simple.

TEACHER: Now listen, there is no class struggle. We must become clear on that subject at once.

SOSTAKOVICH (*getting up*): I can learn nothing from you, if you don't want to know anything about class struggle!

THE MOTHER: You're here to learn reading and writing, and that's something you *can* do here. Reading, too, is class struggle.

TEACHER: What nonsense. What is that supposed to mean; reading is class struggle? What kind of talk is that? (*He writes.*) All right; this means "Worker." Copy it.

THE MOTHER: Do you want to know what "reading is class struggle" means? It means we can put together our own pamphlets and read our own type of books, once we can read and write. Then we can be leaders in the class struggle.

TEACHER: Look here; although I am a teacher, and for twelve years I have taught reading and writing, there is something I want to tell you: I know that everything, at bottom, is nonsense. Books are nonsense. They only help men to become worse and worse. A simple peasant is a better man for, very simply, not having been spoiled by civilization.

THE MOTHER: Now how do you write "Class Struggle"? Pavel Sostakovich, you must put your hand down firmly; otherwise it trembles, and nobody can read your writing.

TEACHER (*writes*): "Class Struggle." (*To* SOSTAKOVICH:) Be sure to write in a straight line, and not over the edge. Whosoever overwrites the margin also oversteps the law. Knowledge has been heaped upon knowledge for generations and generations now, and book after book has been written. As for technical knowledge, we never before had so much. Of what use is it all? We have never been so confused. The entire lot ought to be hurled into the sea at its deepest point —all the books and machines, into the Black Sea. Let us raise a resistance against knowledge! Have you finished? At times I sink into a deep melancholy. At these moments I ask myself, what have the really great thoughts, thoughts that concern not merely the here and now, but rather the eternal, lasting and universal man, what have these to do with class struggle?

SOSTAKOVICH: Ideas like that are useless. While you're so busy sunk in melancholy, you are exploiting us.

THE MOTHER: Pavel Sostakovich, be quiet! Please, can you tell me, how do I write "Exploitation"?

TEACHER: Exploitation. That is a thing you find only in books. Do you imagine I ever exploited anybody?

SOSTAKOVICH: You say that only because you don't get any of the loot.

THE MOTHER (*to* SOSTAKOVICH): Look; the "e" in exploitation is just like the "e" in worker.

TEACHER: Knowledge is of no help. Knowledge helps not at all. What helps is to be good.

THE MOTHER: Well, you just let us have your knowledge if you don't need it.

PRAISE OF LEARNING

Sung by those who are learning

Study from bottom up,
for you who will take the leadership,
it is not too late!
Study the ABC; it is not enough,
but study it! Do not become discouraged,
begin! You must know everything!
You must prepare to take command now!

Study, man in exile!
Study, man in the prison!
Study, wife in your kitchen!
Study, old-age pensioner!
You must prepare to take command now!
Locate yourself a school, homeless folk!
Go search some knowledge, you who freeze!
You who starve, reach for a book:
it will be a weapon.
You must prepare to take command now.

Don't be afraid to question, comrades!
Never believe on faith,
see for yourself!
What you yourself don't learn
you don't know.
Question the reckoning
you yourself must pay it.
Set down your finger on each small item, asking:
where do you get this?
You must prepare to take command now!

THE MOTHER (*getting up*): That will be enough for today. We can't take in as much at one time as we used to. We must be careful not to rob our Pavel Sostakovich of his entire night's sleep again. We do want to thank you, Nicholai Ivanovitch. We can only say that you are helping us very much, when you teach us to read and write.

TEACHER: I find that difficult to believe. I do not wish to maintain, however, that your opinions are totally without sense. In our next lesson I will come back to them.

IVAN VESSOVCHIKOV
FAILS TO RECOGNIZE HIS BROTHER

IVAN: I have been wanting to look in on you, Mrs. Vlassova, and bring you some of our pamphlets. Has Pavel written to you?

THE MOTHER: No; not a line. I am very worried for him.

TEACHER: You have no need to worry about such a man as your son.

THE MOTHER: I never know just what he may be doing or what is being done to him; that is the worst of it. For instance, I don't even know if they give him enough to eat or if maybe he is cold. Do you know if they give them blankets there? He makes me feel very proud. I'm lucky. I have a son who is needed. (*She recites.*)

> Two are too many.
> If others are gone it's best
> but if he's not there he's missed.
>
> He organizes his fight
> around wage levels, water for tea
> and power in the state.

He asks of property:
where do you come from?
He asks of opinions:
to whom are you useful?

Wherever silence is
there will he speak out
and where oppression rules
        and Fate is all the talk
there will he name names.

Where he sits down to table
discontent sits down with him
the food begins to stink
and the room is seen to be cramped.

Wherever they hunt him,
with him goes tumult,
and when they expel him
disquiet stays behind.

IVAN: Ever since their arrest they've been swallowed up like in an earthquake. No one can get to see them. The movement suffers, too, because Pavel is the only one, for instance, who knows the addresses of peasants who want our newspaper. And nothing is more important just now than contacting the landless peasants.

THE MOTHER: I was thinking that, too; we have to go and talk with the peasants.

TEACHER: You would have to talk with a great many people to do that. It's impossible; there are some one hundred and twenty million peasants. Revolution is something you will never have in this country with these people. Russians will never make a revolution. That must be left to the West. Germans, now, there you have real revolutionaries; they'll have a revolution. There's another matter, which I was telling my friend Sakkar about: in the newspapers of these people there is nothing worth reading.

IVAN *laughs.*

What's the matter?

IVAN: Where has your splendid portrait of the Tsar gone? The room looks empty without it.

TEACHER: I simply thought I would put it away for a while. How boring it is always to have it before one. But why won't you tell me why there is nothing in your newspaper concerning school conditions?

IVAN: The way it looks to me—I don't believe you put the picture away just because it's boring.

THE MOTHER: Don't you say that! Nicholai Ivanovitch always is on the lookout for something new.

IVAN: I see.

TEACHER: Be that as it may, I'm less than delighted when I am treated like an idiot. You have been asked a question, about your newspaper.

IVAN: I can't remember, Nicholai, when you ever changed anything in your house. Just the frame must have cost you twelve rubles.

TEACHER: In that case, I can hang the frame up again.

You always considered me a fool; that is why you yourself are a fool.

IVAN: Nicholai Ivanovitch, I am surprised. This provocative talk, and your contemptuous attitude toward our Tsar positively astonish me. It looks like you've become an agitator. Your eyes, too; they've taken on such a masterful glance! Even to look at you is dangerous.

THE MOTHER: Stop making your brother angry! He is a very intelligent man. And it's very important, what he has to say about such matters, since he has many children who learn something from him. Besides, he has helped us to learn reading and writing.

IVAN: Let's hope you managed to learn something yourself, while you were teaching them how to read.

TEACHER: Not at all. I haven't learned a thing. Even now there is very little these poor people understand about Marxism. I have no wish to offend you, Mrs. Vlassova. But Marxism is very naturally a most complicated matter, not at all comprehensible save to the trained mind. What is odd is that the very ones who gulp it down like hot cakes are the ones who will not understand this fact. Marxism has nothing wrong with it, per se. There is even much that can be said for it—though, of course, great deficiencies naturally exist, and at several key points Marx viewed matters completely wrong. I could say much on this subject. The economic aspect is important, granted; but not only the economic aspect is important. Nonetheless, it is important. And what of sociology? As for myself, I must consider, for example, biology to be fully as important. I ask myself where the universal man is in this doctrine. The human being will ever remain the same.

THE MOTHER (*to* IVAN): But *he* already has changed a bit, don't you think?

IVAN: Mrs. Vlassova, I no longer recognize my brother.

7

PRISON

Pelagea Vlassova visits her son in prison, with the purpose of learning the names of peasants who sympathize with the movement.

THE MOTHER: The guard will be paying close attention, but that can't make any difference; I still have to learn the addresses of peasants who want our newspaper. I do hope I can keep all their names in my head.

The GUARD brings Pavel in.

PAVEL: Mama, how are you?

GUARD: You have to be seated so there always is a space between you. There; and there. Conversations about politics are strictly forbidden.

PAVEL: Well; tell me how it is at home, mother!

THE MOTHER: Yes, Pavel.

PAVEL: Are you well looked after?

THE MOTHER: By Vessovchikov, the teacher.

PAVEL: Do they take good care of you?

THE MOTHER: Yes. How are you?

PAVEL: I was worried you might not be well enough looked after.

THE MOTHER: Your beard has gotten so heavy now.

PAVEL: Yes. I look a little older, don't I?

MOTHER: I was at Smilgin's funeral, too. The police got rough again and arrested some. All of us were there.

GUARD: Mrs. Vlassova, that is political!

THE MOTHER: Oh? Really? It's hard to know what a person can talk about!

GUARD: In that case your visit is wasted. Although you have nothing to say, you come running here to bother us. And I'm the one who gets the brunt of it.

PAVEL: Do you help out around the house?

THE MOTHER: That also. Vessovchikov and I plan to go out to the country, next week.

PAVEL: You mean the teacher?

THE MOTHER: No; Ivan.

PAVEL: They want you to have a rest?

MOTHER: That also. (*Softly.*) We need the addresses. (*Aloud.*) Oh, Pavel, we all miss you so.

PAVEL (*softly*): I swallowed the addresses when I was arrested. I only remember a few.

THE MOTHER: Oh, Pavel, I never dreamed I would have to pass my last years like this.

PAVEL (*softly*): Lushin in Pirogovo.

THE MOTHER (*softly*): And in Krapivna? (*Aloud.*) Really, you cause me so much heartache!

PAVEL (*softly*): Sulinovsky.

THE MOTHER: I pray for you, too. (*Softly.*) Sulinovsky in Krapivna. (*Aloud.*) I'm passing the twilight of my life alone, sitting by a lamp.

PAVEL (*softly*): Terek in Tobraya.

THE MOTHER: And the teacher Vessovchikov has begun to complain about the trouble I make him.

PAVEL (*softly*): From them you can get the other addresses.

GUARD: Visiting time is up.

THE MOTHER: Just one moment longer, sir, please. I am so confused. Ah, Pavel, what remains to us old people except to crawl off in some dark corner where no one has to see us—we are no use to anybody. (*Softly.*) Lushin in Pirogovo. (*Aloud.*) They make sure to let us know when our time is past. We have nothing to look forward to. Everything we've learned belongs to the past. (*Softly.*) Sulinovsky in Tobraya.

PAVEL *shakes his head No.*

Sulinovsky in Krapivna (*Aloud.*) And our experience means nothing. The advice we give leads only to harm; there is this deep, unbridgeable gulf between us and our sons. (*Softly.*) Terek in Tobraya. (*Aloud.*) We go one way and you another. (*Softly.*) Terek in

Tobraya. (*Aloud.*) We have nothing in common. The time that is coming is all yours!

GUARD: But the time for visiting is up.

PAVEL: (*makes a bow*): Mother, farewell.

THE MOTHER: (*likewise making a bow*): Farewell, Pavel.

SONG

Sung by the actor who plays Pavel.

They own law books and ordinances
They own prisons and penitentiaries;
their "deterrent measures" we needn't mention!
They own jailers and judges
who are well paid, ready to do anything:
Sure, so what?
    Before they perish (and that will be soon)
    they will see how all they did was in vain.

They own newspapers and printing presses
they use them to attack and to silence us;
their statesmen we needn't mention!
They own priests and professors
who are well paid, ready to do anything:
Sure, so what?
Must they so much fear the truth?
    Before they perish (and that will be soon)
    they will see how all they did was in vain.

They own tanks and cannon
machine guns and hand grenades;
their blackjacks we needn't mention!
They own policemen and soldiers
who are badly paid, ready to do anything.

Sure, so what?
Is their enemy so powerful?
    They say a halt must be called now,
    to hold what's tottering up.
    A day will come, it will come soon
    when they'll see it all was no use.
    Then they can go on screaming "Stop!"
    Neither their money nor cannon will save them!

8

COUNTRY ROAD

Rural agitation.

THE MOTHER *appears in the company of two Workers. She is met with hurled stones. Her companions flee.*

THE MOTHER (*with a large lump on her forehead, to the stone throwers*): Why did you throw stones at us?

YEGOR: Because you're strikebreakers.

THE MOTHER: Oh! so they are strikebreakers. No wonder they are in such a hurry. But where is the strike?

YEGOR: On the Smirnov estate.

THE MOTHER: And you are the strikers? But my bump tells me that. Well, I am not a strikebreaker. I am from Tver; and there is a farm worker I want to see. His name is Yegor Lushin.

YEGOR: Lushin, that's who I am.

THE MOTHER: Pelagea Vlassova. I brought our newspaper for you. I had no idea you were on strike; but I can see (*pointing to the lump on her head*) you are making a strong fight of it.

YEGOR: Please excuse us for giving you that bump. The strike has been going badly. We have no strike fund, and no food; nearly everyone plans to split up tonight, and see what we can do for ourselves on the nearby estates. A whole mob of strikebreakers is coming tomorrow. They've slaughtered the pigs and the calves for them already.

THE MOTHER: Who does the slaughtering?

YEGOR: The butcher on the estate. Naturally, the estate butcher shop, bakery and dairy aren't on strike.

THE MOTHER: But why aren't they striking?

YEGOR: Why should they strike? Only the wages of us who work the land were cut.

THE MOTHER: That means their wages were not cut?

YEGOR: Well, of course they were; but not just now.

THE MOTHER: And you haven't spoken with these people?

YEGOR: It wouldn't help. What is there in common between them and us? Just look, there, how the chimney on the estate kitchen is still smoking—for the strikebreakers. We are peasants and they are workers. Peasants are peasants and workers are workers. What the butcher is, is a worker. He used to work in the canteen of a factory before he got this job.

THE MOTHER: Does that mean he won't strike with you? And meanwhile you have no soup to eat?

YEGOR: Don't puzzle yourself with questions; just let us have those newspapers.

THE MOTHER: Here yours are. (*She makes two bundles of the papers, and gives one to him.*)

YEGOR: What about those? Why don't you give them all to us?

THE MOTHER: The rest are for the estate kitchen.

YEGOR: Do you mean the butcher? He knows very well what he's doing. He won't listen to a thing you can say. He does what he does because if he didn't, he wouldn't eat either. You can't tell such a fellow anything new.

THE MOTHER: Even if he does know it all, that isn't enough. Let me tell you something. I am a worker myself, and I think it is wrong that you haven't spoken with my fellow worker, just because you yourselves know it all already. More than anything else, you have to start with the idea that where there's a worker all is not yet lost. Anyway, I have to take them their newspapers. Even though it really is a shame the estate's kitchen chimney is still smoking so.

(*She hurries off to the estate kitchen.*)

YEGOR: That woman just has no sense. It's people like her who pay no heed to reality. Peasants are peasants and workers are workers.

THE ESTATE KITCHEN

In the estate kitchen, two STRIKEBREAKERS *sit over dinner and talk to the* BUTCHER.

FIRST STRIKEBREAKER (*chewing, to the other*): Anyone who would leave his country in the lurch during the hour of danger is a rat! And that's what a worker who strikes is; someone who leaves his country in the lurch.

BUTCHER (*chopping meat*): What do you mean, his country?

FIRST STRIKEBREAKER: This is Russia, and they are Russians. Russia belongs to the Russians.

BUTCHER: Oh? Really?

SECOND STRIKEBREAKER: You bet. Anyone who can't feel that—my meat's a little raw still—well, you just can't explain it to such people. But you can bash their skulls in.

BUTCHER: Perfectly right!

FIRST STRIKEBREAKER: This table is fatherland. This meat is fatherland.

BUTCHER: But it's a little raw still.

SECOND STRIKEBREAKER: This spot here where I'm sitting is fatherland. And, listen here—(*to the* BUTCHER) you're a hunk of the fatherland too.

BUTCHER: But I'm a little raw too!

FIRST STRIKEBREAKER: A man ought to defend his fatherland.

BUTCHER: That's if it *is* his.

SECOND STRIKEBREAKER: You're just talking that dirty materialism.

BUTCHER: Asshole!

THE MOTHER, *who makes much of the wound on her head, is led in by the* BUTCHER'S WIFE.

BUTCHER'S WIFE: Won't you please have a seat here! I'll make you a cold compress; and you should take something to eat, so you'll get over your shock. (*To the others*:) They threw a stone at her.

FIRST STRIKEBREAKER: Yeah, that's the woman. She rode with us on the train.

SECOND STRIKEBREAKER: It was the strikers who did that to her. We were worried for her.

THE MOTHER: It feels a little better now.

STRIKEBREAKERS: God be thanked!

BUTCHER'S WIFE: How those animals will fight with her over a little piece of work! And such a bruise! (*She goes to get water.*)

THE MOTHER (*to the audience*): How much more sympathy there is for a bruise from people expecting bruises, than from those dealing them out!

FIRST STRIKEBREAKER (*pointing with his fork at* THE MOTHER): Here is a Russian woman struck with stones by Russian workers. Are you a mother?

THE MOTHER: Yes.

FIRST STRIKEBREAKER: A Russian mother struck with stones!

BUTCHER: Yes; Russian stones. (*To the audience*:) And I have to serve my good soup to this bunch. (*To* THE MOTHER:) Why did they throw them at you?

THE MOTHER (*cooling the bruise with a wet rag*): Because they saw me walking with strikebreakers.

SECOND STRIKEBREAKER: What a bunch of rats they are.

THE MOTHER: What do you mean, rats? Do you know what I was just thinking? That maybe they're not rats, at all.

BUTCHER'S WIFE: If they're not then why did they throw stones at you?

THE MOTHER: Because they thought I was a rat.

BUTCHER'S WIFE: How could they ever think that?

THE MOTHER: They thought I was a strikebreaker.

BUTCHER (*smiles*): Then you think we should throw stones at strikebreakers?

THE MOTHER: Well, certainly.

BUTCHER (*beaming, to his wife*): Let her have some food! Give her something right away! Two plates full! (*He goes to* THE MOTHER.) My name is Vassil Yefimovitch. (*Calling to his wife.*) And bring in the help! I want them to see this.

The help enters through the door.

This woman was stoned by the strikers. She has a bruise on her head. See, here it is. Just now I asked her, where did she get the bruise. She says, They took me for a strikebreaker. I ask, Do you mean we should throw stones at strikebreakers? And what do you suppose she said?

THE MOTHER: Yes.

BUTCHER: As soon as I heard that, dear friends, I said: Give her some food! Two plates full! (*To* THE

MOTHER:) But why don't you eat it? Is it too hot for you? (*To his wife*:) Why did you have to set steaming hot food before her? Do you want her to burn her mouth?

THE MOTHER (*shoving the plate away*): No, Vassil Yefimovitch, the food is not too hot.

BUTCHER: Then why don't you eat it?

THE MOTHER: Because it was cooked for strikebreakers.

BUTCHER: What did you say?

THE MOTHER: It was cooked for strikebreakers.

BUTCHER: Well! That's a new one! This is getting interesting. That makes me a rat too, doesn't it? Look at me —I'm a rat! And why am I a rat? Because I give support to strikebreakers. (*To* THE MOTHER:) Isn't that right? (*He sits down with her.*) But isn't it wrong to strike? Or do you think it all depends upon the reason for the strike?

THE MOTHER *nods*.

What you mean is, the pay was cut. But why do you think the pay can't be cut? Just have a look—all you can see out there, it all belongs to Mr. Smirnov who lives in Odessa. And why shouldn't he cut the wages?

The STRIKEBREAKERS *agree heartily*.

Isn't it his money? Maybe you don't believe he can set wages one time at two rubles, another time at two kopeks? What—you don't believe that either? Well, but what happened just last year? My wages were cut too, even that! And what did I do—(*to his wife*) on your advice? Nothing! And what will happen in September? My pay will be cut again! So what am I making myself guilty of now? Of treason; treason to people whose pay was cut too, and who didn't go along with it. What does this make me, then? (*To* THE MOTHER:) So you won't eat my food? I've been waiting for a respectable human being to tell me to my face that as a respectable human being he can't eat my food. Now the cup is full. The cup has been full a long time. It needed just a drop—(*he points at Vlassova*) for it to run over. Anger and discontent are not enough. So—a thing must have practical results. (*To the* STRIKEBREAKERS:) You tell your Mr. Smirnov he can send up your food from Odessa. And you can cook it yourselves, the pig.

BUTCHER'S WIFE: Now don't you get all worked up.

BUTCHER: It wasn't for nothing that I cooked in factory canteens. It was because I couldn't take the crap I got out of them.

His wife tries to calm him.

I told myself, I will go into the country, it's decent there; and what do I find? Another dungheap, and I'm supposed to stuff my food into strikebreakers.

BUTCHER'S WIFE: We can move back there again.

BUTCHER: Damn right, we are moving. (*Grandly.*) Bring in the kettle of lentils. And you; get all the bacon. Whatever you can find! What's it been cooked for?

BUTCHER'S WIFE: You're going to be sorry! You'll bring us to a bad end yet.

BUTCHER (*to the* STRIKEBREAKERS): Get out of here, you
saviors of the fatherland! We're on strike. The kitchen
help is striking. Out! (*He drives the* STRIKEBREAKERS
out.) As a butcher, I've gotten into the habit of being
the one who laughs last, and not the pig. (*He goes
to stand before* THE MOTHER, *with his arm around his
wife's shoulder.*) And now, go and tell the ones who
stoned you that their soup's waiting.

PRAISE FOR THE VLASSOVAS

Recited by the Butcher and his Helpers.

Here is our comrade Vlassova, a good fighter.
Hardworking, clever and reliable.
Reliable in the fight. Clever against our enemy, and
hardworking in her agitation. Her work is small,
tenaciously done, and indispensable.
Wherever she fights, she is not alone.
Others like her fight tenaciously, reliably, cleverly
in Tver, Glasgow, Lyon and Chicago
Shanghai and Calcutta
all the Vlassovas of all countries, good small moles
unknown soldiers of the revolution,
indispensable.

9

HOME OF THE
TEACHER, VESSOVCHIKOV

The return of PAVEL.

Pelagea Vlassova and two Workers carry a printing press into the home of the teacher Vessovchikov.

TEACHER: Pelagea Vlassova, you cannot set up a printing press here in my house. You are abusing my sympathy for the movement. You know I am for you, theoretically, but this is going much too far.

THE MOTHER: Did I understand you right, Nicholai Ivanovitch, that you are in favor of our pamphlets? You yourself drew up the last one for the Workers' Alliance, I might remind you. And yet you don't want them printed?

They are setting up the machine.

TEACHER: Well, I do. But printing them here, that I can't have.

THE MOTHER (*offended*): We make note of this, Nicholai Ivanovitch.

They continue working.

TEACHER: And what if you do?

FIRST WORKER: Once Mrs. Vlassova has something in her head, there's no stopping her. We've had scruples about this, so far as we're concerned. But nothing comes of it. By eight o'clock the paper has to be ready.

THE MOTHER: We have to print more newspapers now; they keep confiscating them. Just when the oppression gets strongest is when people turn indifferent and pretend they're happy with all the dirt and meanness.

The TEACHER *goes to the next room and reads.*

They begin printing; the machine makes a terrific noise. The TEACHER *rushes in.*

THE MOTHER: It's a little loud; don't you think?

TEACHER: My lamp fell off the table! If it's going to make such a racket, I cannot let you print illegal publications here!

THE MOTHER: We've noticed it too, Nicholai Ivanovitch. The machine is a bit loud.

SECOND WORKER: If only we had something to put under it, the next-door apartments wouldn't hear a thing. Do you have anything to put under it, Nicholai Ivanovitch?

TEACHER: No, I haven't anything.

THE MOTHER: Don't make such a noise!—Our neighbor has a piece of felt in her closet; she's saving it to make her children some coats. I'll ask her for it. Don't print while I'm gone. (*She goes to the neighbor.*)

FIRST WORKER (*to the* TEACHER): Please don't be angry

with her. Actually it's us who brought her here so she could feel at peace with her politics. We didn't want to involve her in illegal printing work. But she wouldn't have it any other way.

A knock. They hide the machine. The TEACHER *opens.*

PAVEL'S VOICE (*from outside*): Does Pelagea Vlassova live here? My name is Pavel Vlassov.

PAVEL *enters.*

PAVEL: How do you do. Where is my mother?

SECOND WORKER: She'll be back in a minute. Are they after you?

PAVEL: Yes; that also. I have to go on to Finland, tonight.

FIRST WORKER: Sit down over here. Let's give your mother a big surprise.

They place PAVEL *in a chair facing the door, and station themselves around him.* THE MOTHER *enters.*

THE MOTHER: Pavel! (*She embraces him.*) You get thinner and thinner! Instead of fatter he gets thinner! I knew they wouldn't keep you for long. How did you get away? How long can you stay here?

PAVEL: I have to go on to Finland, tonight.

SECOND WORKER: Did you get the felt? (*To* PAVEL:) We have to be ready with the newspapers by eight o'clock.

PAVEL: Then print away!

THE MOTHER (*beaming*): Start in with the printing, so we can have more time. What do you think of this; that Marfa Katerinovna tossed my request right back in my face! And why? The felt is for coats for her children. I say: "Marfa Katerinovna, just now I saw your children coming from school. In coats!" "Coats," she says, "those aren't coats, those are patched-up rags. All the other schoolchildren laugh at them." "Marfa Katerinovna," I say, "it's the way with poor people to have ragged coats. Just let me have your felt until tomorrow morning. Let me tell you, it will help your children more if you let me have it than a fancy coat would." But you have never seen such stubbornness, that no good! She really would not give it to me. Not even for a promise of two kopeks! (*From under her apron she takes a few pieces of felt and sets them under the machine.*)

TEACHER: In that case, what's this?

THE MOTHER: The felt, naturally!

All laugh.

SECOND WORKER: But why do you go on complaining about this Marfa Katerinovna, then?

THE MOTHER: Because she made me steal it, since we absolutely had to have it. It's a very good thing for her children that papers like ours are printed. That's the pure and simple truth!

SECOND WORKER: We thank you in the name of the revolution, Pelagea Vlassova, for this felt!

Laughter.

THE MOTHER: I'll give it back to her tomorrow. (*To* PAVEL, *who has sat down.*) Don't you want some bread with butter?

SECOND WORKER (*at the machine*): And who will take the pages out of the machine?

THE MOTHER *takes her post at the machine.* PAVEL *gets his own bread.*

THE MOTHER: Look in the cupboard below. The knife is in the drawer.

PAVEL: Don't worry about me! I was able to find a slice of bread even in Siberia.

THE MOTHER: Do you hear him? He's blaming me. I don't pay attention to him. The least I can do is cut that bread for you.

TEACHER: And who will take the pages out of the machine?

PAVEL (*cutting a slice of bread from the loaf while the others continue to print*): The mother of the revolutionist Pavel Vlassov takes the pages out. Does she pay any attention to him? Not at all! Does she make him his tea? Does she run his bath water? Or kill the fatted calf? Not at all! He flees from Siberia toward Finland, the icy gusts of the North wind in his face, the volleys of the gendarmes in his ears, and he finds no sanctuary where he might lay his head down—save in a printshop. And instead of bending over him to stroke his hair, his mother is taking the pages out!

THE MOTHER: If you want to help me, come here.

PAVEL *takes his place opposite* THE MOTHER *at the printing machine.*

They recite.

THE MOTHER: Has it gone badly with you?

PAVEL: Everything was fine, until the typhus epidemic came.

THE MOTHER: Anyhow, have you always been able to eat properly?

PAVEL: Yes, until there was nothing.

THE MOTHER: Where are you going now? Will you be gone long?

PAVEL: No; if you here work like this.

THE MOTHER: Will you be working too, there?

PAVEL: Of course, and it is equally important, there and here.

A knock. SOSTAKOVICH *enters.*

SOSTAKOVICH: You must go at once, Pavel. Here are your tickets. Comrade Issay waits for you at the railroad station; he has your Finnish passport.

PAVEL: I hoped at least I would have a few hours. But it doesn't matter.

THE MOTHER (*getting her coat*): I'll go with you down there.

SOSTAKOVICH: No, that's dangerous for Pavel. You're known, he's not!

PAVEL: Until next time then, mother!

THE MOTHER: The next time, let's hope I can fix you the bread and butter.

PAVEL: Good-bye, comrades!

PAVEL *and* SOSTAKOVICH *leave.*

TEACHER: God goes with him, Vlassova.

THE MOTHER: I'm not so sure.

THE MOTHER *returns to the machine. They continue printing.*

THE MOTHER (*recites*):

PRAISE FOR THE COMMON CAUSE

How often you hear
how quickly the mothers lose their sons;
but I have kept my son.
How have I kept him? Through a third, the cause.
He and I were two; the third it was,
the common cause commonly driving us, that is what
united us.
How often I myself have heard
sons, talking with their parents.
But how much better our talks were,
about the third, that cause, which we held in common,
for many people the great and common cause!
How close we felt to each other, this cause near.
How good we were for each other,
this good cause near.

10

GENERAL STORE

THE MOTHER *attempts to combat the indifference shown by the exploited toward their sufferings, even in trivial everyday events. The Coat of Paper.*

WOMAN WORKER (*with a child*): What does it all come to?

SHOPMISTRESS: The sausages are five, the flour twelve, the jam is ten, the tea is twenty, and matches are two kopeks. That's forty-nine kopeks total.

WOMAN WORKER (*to the child*): See that, Ilyitch, forty-nine kopeks, and I have still to buy you a coat. (*To the other women in the store*:) He always seems to be cold.

WOMEN: He's gotten much too thin. No wonder he catches cold. How can you let him run around like that, when it's snowing so much?

WOMAN WORKER: Oh, but I have only twenty kopeks left. Do you have coats for that much?

The SHOPMISTRESS *points at a rack where six children's coats hang.*

WOMAN WORKER: Well, you have a good selection. (*She examines the material.*) This one is the right size. But the other, there, isn't so expensive. Of course it's

106

not so warm either. But it's not so bad. The one with the lining would be better.

SHOPMISTRESS: It costs more, too.

WOMAN WORKER: How much does the thin one cost?

SHOPMISTRESS: Five and a half rubles.

WOMAN WORKER: In that case, I can't buy it. I haven't that much money.

SHOPMISTRESS: It costs nothing to die, you know. (*To another woman*:) May I help you?

WOMAN: A half pound of grits.

WOMAN WORKER: You see, what happened is they cut the wages again down at the Muratov Works, several weeks back.

THE MOTHER: I also heard that the workers agreed to it.

WOMAN WORKER: But only because Mr. Muratov would have closed down the factory otherwise. If I'm forced to choose between getting paid less and seeing the factory closed down, I'll take a lower wage.

THE MOTHER: Ilyitch, do you see that; you always have to pick the lesser evil. In the end it's the lesser evil for Mr. Muratov, too. He would rather pay us less than more. Ilyitch darling, if Mr. Muratov wants to make his profit he has to cut your daddy's wages. Of course, if your daddy doesn't want to go on working, he doesn't have to. But you do need a coat. Surely you don't need a twenty kopeks coat; but you must have a coat. Now, if a twenty kopeks coat were what he needed, this would be his coat.

She takes a paper pattern from the counter and holds it up to little Ilyitch.

SHOPMISTRESS: Put my pattern back where you got it from.

FIRST WOMAN: Oh, it's only a joke.

SECOND WOMAN: But why must you mock the child?

THE MOTHER: Who is it who mocks Ilyitch? I, or Mr. Muratov and the coat manufacturer? Ilyitch requires a coat for a few kopeks; and he has gotten the coat. Are you saying it's not warm? Then a warm coat is what he should have required!

SHOPMISTRESS: What you want to say is that I'm guilty because I don't give her a coat as a gift.

WOMAN WORKER: I don't demand anything of you. I know you can't do anything like that.

FIRST WOMAN (*to* THE MOTHER): Did you really mean that the shopmistress is guilty?

THE MOTHER: No. The only guilty person is Ilyitch.

WOMAN WORKER: Anyway, I won't be able to buy the coat.

SHOPMISTRESS: It isn't right for you to buy, if the price is too much for you.

THE MOTHER: That's right, Ilyitch. You don't need a coat at all if the price is too high.

WOMAN WORKER: All I have is twenty kopeks left; no more.

SECOND WOMAN: I recognize this woman. She goes around everywhere, sowing discontent.

FIRST WOMAN (*indicating the* SHOPMISTRESS, *who has begun to cry*): She has got to pay the manufacturers for the coats.

THE MOTHER: But this isn't a coat, of course—it's not warm. And those (*pointing at the six coats on the rack*) aren't coats either—those are merchandise. But Ilyitch can't buy any other coat if the coat manufacturer is going to get his profit. Ilyitch, this coat is the lesser evil. Supposing you had none at all, that would be the greater evil. So now go outside in your little coat, Ilyitch; and tell the snow it has to protect you, since Mr. Muratov will not protect you. Your coat is wrong, Ilyitch, and you have the wrong parents—they haven't the slightest idea of how to get coats for you. Now go and tell the snow and the wind that right here is where they should snow; for here is where the coats hang.

11

HOME OF THE
TEACHER, VESSOVCHIKOV

CHORUS

Sung to THE MOTHER **by** *Revolutionary Workers*

Comrade Vlassova, your son
has been shot. But when
he went to the wall to be shot
he went to a wall made by men like himself
and men like himself
made the weapons aimed at his breast, and the bullets.
They had gone elsewhere
or were fled elsewhere, yet in his eyes
were present by the work of their hands.
Even those who shot at him
were not different from him, nor forever unteachable.
Although he went in chains
still forged by his comrades and bound about him
     by comrades,
he saw while they took him
how the factories grew more dense, chimney by chimney,
and, since it was dawn—
the usual time for leading them out—
the factories still stood empty, but he saw them filled
with that mighty force which ever had grown
and grew still.

Three WOMEN *enter, bringing a Bible and a kettle
of food.*

WOMEN (*outside the door*): They caught Pavel Vlassov when he tried to cross into Finland; and they shot him. We are going to forget all our quarrels with Mrs. Vlassova, and just sit down with her like Christians to show her our sympathy. Since she doesn't believe in anything, she must be inconsolable in her great misery. (*They enter.*)

LANDLADY: You are not alone in these difficult days, Mrs. Vlassova. The entire house suffers with you.

The three WOMEN *are overcome with feeling and sit down. They sob loudly.*

THE MOTHER (*after a while*): Please take a little tea. It will refresh you.

She pours out tea for them.

THE MOTHER: Do you feel better, now?

LANDLADY: You are so composed, Mrs. Vlassova.

SECOND WOMAN: But you are perfectly right. We are all of us in God's hands.

THIRD WOMAN: And God knows what He does.

THE MOTHER *says nothing.*

THIRD WOMAN: We just thought we might be able to do something for you. No doubt the things you have been up to, of late, are nothing proper. Now here's a kettle of food, you need only warm it up.

She gives her the kettle.

THE MOTHER: Many thanks, Lydia Antonovna. It is a great kindness of you to have thought of it. And really, it is most friendly of you all to have come.

LANDLADY: Dear Vlassova, I've also brought along my Bible in case you want to do some reading. You may keep it as long as you like.

She holds out the Bible to THE MOTHER.

THE MOTHER: Vera Stefanovna, I thank you for your good intention. But will you be terribly offended if I give the book back to you? The teacher Vessovchikov left me his books to use when he went away on vacation.

She returns the Bible.

LANDLADY: It seemed to me that you won't want to read those political newspapers of yours now.

SECOND WOMAN: Really, do you read them every day?

THE MOTHER: Yes.

LANDLADY: My Bible often has been a great consolation to me, Mrs. Vlassova.

Silence.

THIRD WOMAN: Haven't you any photographs of him?

THE MOTHER: No. I had a few. But then we destroyed them all, so the police couldn't get their hands on them.

THIRD WOMAN: A person should have things like that for remembrance.

SECOND WOMAN: They say he was such a fine man!

THE MOTHER: I remember now, I do have a photograph.
This is the warrant for his arrest. He cut it out of a
newspaper for me.

The WOMEN *look at the warrant.*

LANDLADY: It says here in black and white, Mrs. Vlassova,
that your son was a criminal. He never had a belief,
and you make no secret of being the same way. I
might even add you take every opportunity to let us
know what you think of our faith.

THE MOTHER: Yes—nothing, Vera Stefanovna.

LANDLADY: And you haven't yet come to another conviction?

THE MOTHER: No, Vera Stefanovna.

LANDLADY: Can you still believe that the reason alone
will accomplish everything?

THIRD WOMAN: Vera Stefanovna, I told you that Mrs.
Vlassova surely wouldn't have changed her view for
yours.

LANDLADY: But not long ago, in the night, I heard through
the wall how you were weeping.

THE MOTHER: I hope you can excuse me.

LANDLADY: You have no need to excuse yourself. That
naturally isn't how I meant it. But did you weep
because of reason?

THE MOTHER: No.

LANDLADY: Now you see just how far you get with your reason.

THE MOTHER: It wasn't because of reason that I wept. But when I stopped weeping, that was not because of unreasonableness. What Pavel has done was good.

LANDLADY: Why was he shot, then?

THIRD WOMAN: Because all of them were against him?

THE MOTHER: Yes; but when they were against him, they were also against themselves.

LANDLADY: Mankind needs God, Pelagea Vlassova. We are helpless against fate.

THE MOTHER: What we say is this: the fate of man is man.

SECOND WOMAN: Dear Mrs. Vlassova, we peasants—

LANDLADY (*pointing to her*): My relative. She's just visiting here.

SECOND WOMAN: We who are peasants think otherwise. Here, there is no seed in the field, only a loaf of bread in the breadbox. You see only the milk; you do not see the cow. You have no idea of those sleepless nights with a thunderstorm up there in the heavens; and what is the meaning of hail to you?

THE MOTHER: I understand. And in these situations you pray to God?

SECOND WOMAN: Yes.

THE MOTHER: And in the spring, you go on processions and pilgrimages?

SECOND WOMAN: That's right.

THE MOTHER: And then the thunderstorms come, and then it hails. And in spite of everything the cow gets sick. Aren't there any peasants yet in your region who have insurance against crop failure and cattle disease?

SECOND WOMAN: I hear that there are.

THE MOTHER: Well, when the praying does no good, insurance does help. That's how it is. You have no need to pray to God any more when the thunderclouds stand overhead; but you must be insured. That will help you. And if God loses his importance, well, that is too bad for God. Which gives reason to hope that once this God has disappeared from your fields he will disappear out of your heads too. When I was young, everyone was still positive that He was sitting somewhere up in Heaven and looked like an old man. Then, airplanes came, and in the newspapers you could read that everything in the heavens could now be measured. People stopped talking about a God who sits in Heaven. They began to talk about the idea that He was a sort of gas, nowhere, yet everywhere. But as soon as you read what the gasses composing everything were made of, God wasn't there either. We understood what the air was; so He couldn't go on being like air. That's the way He got more and more dispersed, until, you might say, He just evaporated. They tell us nowadays that He's actually just a spiritual symbol—but even that is very doubtful, Lydia Antonovna.

THIRD WOMAN: Are you saying He's not so important any more because we can't see any sign of Him?

LANDLADY: Mrs. Vlassova, don't you forget why God has taken your Pavel from you.

THE MOTHER: Oh no; it was the Tsar, the Tsar is who took him from me. And I don't forget why, either.

LANDLADY: God took him, not the Tsar.

THE MOTHER: Lydia Antonovna, as I hear it, the God who took my Pavel from me is now planning to take your two rooms away from you, come next Saturday. Is that true? Has God given your eviction notice?

LANDLADY: It was I who gave her notice. She hasn't paid her rent for three times running.

THE MOTHER: Vera Stefanovna, God has ordained that you should not get those three rent payments; now what have you done about it?

Vera Stefanovna is silent.

What you did was to give Lydia Antonovna her eviction notice and throw her out into the street. and you, Lydia Antonovna: What did you do when God so ordained that you should be put onto the street? Perhaps you ought to ask our landlady to lend you her Bible. Then you can leaf through it and read to your children about how we must fear God, while you sit there in the street in the cold.

LANDLADY: Your son would still be living today if you had read more to him from the Bible.

THE MOTHER: Living, perhaps; but living very badly. Why
is it you fear only death? My son had no such great
fear of death. (*She recites.*)

But he shuddered much at the misery
in our cities, apparent to every eye.
Hunger is what shocked us, and the degradation
of those who notice it, and cause it.
Do not fear death so much, but rather the inadequate
life!

Lydia Antonovna, what good does it do you to fear
God? You should fear Vera Stefanovna instead. It
was not the inscrutable will of God which carried
my son Pavel off, but the clear will of the Tsar;
just as Vera Stefanovna has thrown you into the
street because some man who sits in his villa and
lacks all trace of godliness has chased you from your
job. Why speak of God? Although they say there
are many mansions in "our Father's house," there
are certainly too few in Russia. But that they never
tell you, and they don't tell you why.

THIRD WOMAN: Vera Stefanovna, let me have the Bible
for a moment. In the Bible it says very clearly, "Love
Thy Neighbor." Why are you throwing me out onto
the street, then? Let me see the Bible; I'll show it
to you. They shot Pavel Vlassov because he was for
the workers and was a worker himself; that's clear
enough!

LANDLADY: Not for that reason you won't get the Bible
from me; not for that reason!

THIRD WOMAN: Your God does me no good if I can't
see any signs of Him!

She tries to seize the Bible from the LANDLADY.

THIRD WOMAN (*holding fast to the Bible*): For what reason then? Surely not for any good one! Just let me have that book, I'll show you. . . .

LANDLADY: This is my property.

THIRD WOMAN: Yes, just like the whole house, right?

LANDLADY: Now I am going to look up something for you, the section about laying violent hands on another person's property.

The Bible is torn to shreds.

SECOND WOMAN (*picking up the pieces of the Bible*): Now it's been torn apart.

THE MOTHER (*who has protected the kettle of food*): Better the Bible torn apart than the food spilled.

THIRD WOMAN: I would join Pelagea Vlassova's party this very day, if I didn't have faith there is a God in Heaven who rewards everything, both bad and good! (*Exit.*)

LANDLADY: Pelagea Vlassova, you see what you have done to Lydia Antonovna. Your son was shot because he talked like you, and you don't deserve anything better.

She leaves with her relative.

THE MOTHER: You unhappy people! (*Calling after them:*) But anyway—I suggest you take out insurance on your crops! (*She falls down.*)

12

STREET CORNER

1914—The Outbreak of War

THE MOTHER, *brutally beaten, is carried by several* WORK-ERS *behind the shelter of a house.*

FIRST WORKER: What happened to her?

SECOND WORKER: We see this old woman in the middle of the crowd that's cheering the troops off to war. She shouts out: "Down with the war! Long live the revolution!" Then the police come along and club her on the head. We pulled her over here behind this house right away. You—wash off her face.

WORKERS: Run along now, old lady, before they throw you in jail!

THE MOTHER: What happened to my purse?

WORKERS: Here it is!

THE MOTHER: I have some leaflets, here in my purse. You'll read the truth in them about the situation of us workers in the war. It gives the truth here.

WORKERS: Go on home, old lady. Keep the truth tight in your purse! It's too dangerous. We'll be beaten and locked up too, if they catch you here with us. Haven't you had enough?

THE MOTHER: No, no, you have to know what's in these!
  It's our ignorance about the spot we're in that keeps
  us down.

WORKERS: You're forgetting the police.

THE MOTHER: They're also ignorant men.

WORKERS: But what our leaders tell us is that we have
  to beat the Germans and defend our country, first.

THE MOTHER: Is that right? What kind of leaders are these?

  Do you fight side by side with your class enemies,
  workers against workers?
  The organizations you won with hardship
  by pennies of self-denial will be smashed.
  All your experience is forgotten
  and forgotten the solidarity of workers of all lands
  in common fight against the class enemy.

WORKERS: All that means nothing now. In some factories
  we did stage strikes against the war. The strikes were
  completely smashed. There won't be any revolution.
  Go home, old lady. See the world as it is. What you're
  after will never happen; never! never!

THE MOTHER: At least won't you read what we say about
  the situation? Won't you? (*She offers the leaflets.*)
  You don't want to read them?

WORKERS: Your intentions are good—we can tell that—
  but we just don't want your leaflets any more. We
  don't want any more trouble.

THE MOTHER: Y-y-yesss, but think of it: all the world—

(*she shouts, so the frightened* WORKERS *clap their hands over her mouth*) is living in terrible darkness, it's waited till now for you alone, you who could still be reached by reason. Just think, if you refuse!

13

HOME OF THE TEACHER

THE MOTHER *is in sickbed when the news comes that the party is in danger.*

The TEACHER *takes a* DOCTOR *into the room where* THE MOTHER *lies.*

TEACHER: She was in the crowd and was knocked down. Please do not mention the question of fees to her. I will take care of that. (*To* THE MOTHER) Don't be frightened, Mrs. Vlassova. I asked the doctor to come. I'm disturbed about your heavy breathing.

The DOCTOR *examines* THE MOTHER.

THE MOTHER: Did anyone tell you that I have no money?

The DOCTOR *nods.*

DOCTOR (*outside again, with a shrug, to the* TEACHER): She was hit very badly; and she is an old woman.

He leaves. The TEACHER *sits on the bed.*

THE MOTHER: What do the newspapers say?

TEACHER: They have declared martial law. The five delegates to the Duma that you people had were arrested. They've been sent to Siberia, on charges of high treason. I'll go downstairs and buy the latest extra. They are out to destroy your party now.

He leaves.

CHORUS

Sung to THE MOTHER

Get up; the party is in danger!
You are sick, but the party is dying.
You are weak, but we need your help!
Get up; the party is in danger!

You had some doubts about us;
Doubt no longer now,
We're at the end.
You have scolded the party;
Scold the party no longer,
It will be destroyed.

Get up; the party is in danger!
Get up quickly!
You are sick, but you are needed.
Don't die; you must help us.
Don't stay away; we're going into battle.
Get up, the party is in danger, get up!

During this Chorus, THE MOTHER *has laboriously gotten up, dressed, taken her purse, and, uncertainly, but with gathering strength, crossed the room and gone out through the door.*

14

A PATRIOTIC COPPER
COLLECTION DEPOT

THE MOTHER *carries on anti-war propaganda.*

Seven women bearing copper implements—among them,
THE MOTHER *with a small cup—stand before a door
decorated with a flag and the inscription: Patriotic Copper
Collection Depot. An* OFFICIAL *in civilian garb comes and
opens the door.*

OFFICIAL: It has just been announced that our brave
troops, with exemplary heroism, have wrested the
fortress of Przemysl from the enemy for the fourth
time. 100,000 dead; 2,000 prisoners. By order of the
Army High Command, all schools will be closed
and the bells will be sounded. Long live our Holy
Russia; forever! and ever! and ever! The counter
for turning in your copper quota will be open in five
minutes.

He exits.

WOMAN: How wonderful that our war is going so well!

THE MOTHER: I have only this little cup. It won't make
more than five, at the most six cartridges. And of
those, how many do you suppose will hit their mark?
Of six, perhaps two; and of the two, at most one
will be fatal. That kettle of yours is good for twenty

124

cartridges, at least; and the mug that lady up in front has is good for a grenade. One grenade can wipe out five or six men all at once! (*She counts the implements.*) One, two, three, four, five, six, seven; no, wait, the lady brought two, so it's eight then. Eight! That's all it takes to outfit a fine little surprise attack. (*She laughs softly.*) And to think I almost didn't come with my little cup. I met two soldiers on the way—someone really ought to find out who they were—they said to me, "sure, go on, you old goat, turn in your copper so the war won't ever come to an end!" Can you imagine? Isn't that terrible? "You," I said to them, "you deserve to be shot dead. If all I get out of turning in my little cup," I told them, "is that someone fills those dirty mouths of yours, well, I won't have given up my cup for nothing. All it will take is two cartridges." After all— why should I, Pelagea Vlassova, be turning in my copper cup? I am doing it so the war will not end!

WOMAN: What are you talking about? If we turn in our copper the war will not end? The only reason we turn it in is so the war will end!

THE MOTHER: No; we're turning it in so it won't end!

WOMAN IN BLACK: No, that's wrong. If they have copper and can make more grenades then they'll win more quickly over there. Then the war can stop!

THE MOTHER: But don't you see, if they have more grenades then it most certainly won't end, because then they'll be able to keep on with it. So long as they've got ammunition they'll keep going. You mustn't forget the other side makes its collections too.

WOMAN (*pointing at a sign*): "When you turn in your copper you shorten the war!" Can't you read?

THE MOTHER: When you turn in your copper you lengthen the war! That's only for spies!

WOMAN IN BLACK: But whatever reason can you have for wanting the war lengthened?

THE MOTHER: Well, in half a year my son will make sergeant. Just two more assaults, and then my son's a sergeant. We'll get twice as much pay then. Also we have to get hold of Armenia and Galicia; and Turkey we really need.

WOMAN IN BLACK: What do we need?

THE MOTHER: Turkey. And that money we got from France, that has to be paid back somehow too. To this extent it's a war of liberation.

WOMAN: Of course. Certainly this is a war of liberation. But does that mean it has to last into all eternity?

THE MOTHER: Well, it has to last at least another half year.

WOMAN IN BLACK: Do you think it will last that long when they have copper again?

THE MOTHER: Yes; no doubt about it. If it didn't, the soldiers would be fighting for nothing. Have you a son over there too? Well, look; already your son is there, and now you give your copper too. It will go on at least another half year, at this rate.

WOMAN IN BLACK: I don't understand a thing any more. At first I hear the war will be shortened; then that it will be longer. What can a person believe? I've lost my husband already; and my son is now at the gates of Przemysl. I'm going home. (*Exit.*)

The bells begin to sound.

WOMAN: Victory bells!

WOMAN WORKER: You didn't need to say that to her, you know, about wanting the war to go on. There isn't another soul who wants that!

THE MOTHER: No? What about the Tsar? And his generals? You don't think they're afraid of fighting the Germans? What they say is: Keep after the enemy! Victory or death! And that's how it should be. Don't you hear the bells? The bells ring for only two things; a victory, or a death. And why should you be against the war? Who are you, exactly? All of us here are of the decent, better sort, if I am not mistaken. But you look like a worker. Are you or are you not a worker? I am waiting for your reply. Here you are, trying to slip yourself into our midst! Don't you ever forget there is a distance between your type of people and us!

HOUSEMAID: You shouldn't say that to her. She makes sacrifices for the fatherland too.

THE MOTHER (*to the* WOMAN WORKER): How can you possibly stand there with all your heart? What good does the war do you? Sheer hypocrisy and nothing else brings you here. We can get along very well without you and your likes. This is our war! Nobody has anything against you workers having a part, too, but that doesn't mean you belong. Go on back to your factory now—and see to it you get better wages and don't come slipping in here where you don't belong. (*To the* HOUSEMAID.) You can take those patched old pots off her hands, if she absolutely insists on turning them in.

The WOMAN WORKER *runs off.*

THIRD WOMAN: Who is this person who carries on with the big words?

FOURTH WOMAN: I've been listening now for half an hour to the way she drives people away.

THIRD WOMAN: Do you know what this is? A Bolshevik!

WOMEN: What, do you think so?—I know it's a Bolshevik. And a very cunning person indeed!—Just leave her alone and pay no attention to her! We have to protect ourselves against Bolshevism, it has a thousand faces!—If a policeman comes along, he'll simply take her away!

THE MOTHER: Yes, I am a Bolshevik. And you are all murderers; every one of you as you stand there! There is no animal that would sacrifice its young, the way you do yours—without sense or reason and for a rotten cause. You should have the wombs torn out of you. They should wither and you turn sterile, just as you stand there. Why should your sons come back? To such mothers! They're off shooting for a bad cause and should be shot for a bad cause. But you are the murderers.

FIRST WOMAN (*turning around*): I'll give you what you have coming, you Bolshevik!

She advances on THE MOTHER, *the mug in her hand, and beats her about the face. Another* WOMAN *similarly turns and spits. At this point, the counter is opened and the three* WOMEN *go in.*

HOUSEMAID (*who has remained*): You mustn't take it to heart. But I want you to tell me what I should do.

You Bolsheviks are against the war, I know that, but I can't go back to my employers with these copper kettles. I don't want to turn them in. But if I don't turn them in, I won't have helped anybody and I will have lost my job. What should I do, do you think?

THE MOTHER: Alone, there is nothing you can do. Turn in the copper kettles as your masters told you. Your masters will tell people like you to make ammunition out of them. People like you will use them for shooting, too. But, people like you will also decide—at whom to shoot! Tonight, come to (*she whispers the address in her ear*). There will be a worker from the Putilov Works there to speak; and we can explain just how we plan to behave. Be sure not to tell the address to anyone who shouldn't know it.

15

STREET

At the head of a demonstration, THE MOTHER *carries the red flag. At her side marches the* HOUSEMAID.

WORKER: There were already many thousands of us as we crossed over the Lybin Prospect. About fifty factories were on strike, and the strikers joined our ranks in demonstration against the war and against the Tsarist rule.

SECOND WORKER: Some 250,000 men in the factories were striking as early as the winter of 1916-1917. They were brought over to us Bolsheviks by the poor wages, the climbing prices, the lack of basic essentials, the despair over the war, and the way they pushed the hungry workers and peasants out onto the fields of slaughter.

THIRD WORKER: We carried posters that said: "Down with the war! Long live the revolution!" and our red flags.

THE MOTHER: You see, there is still so much that I have to do, I, Pelagea Vlassova, the widow of a worker and the mother of a worker. I was disturbed many years ago to see how my son was not satisfied; at first I only felt despair. But that did no good. Then I helped him in his fight for the kopek. We were involved at the time in small strikes for better wages. Now we are in the midst of a huge strike in the ammunition factories, and we're fighting for power in the state.

HOUSEMAID: Many people say what we want will never happen. We should be content with what we have. Anyway, the power of the ruling class is absolute. Time after time we will be beaten down. Many workers also say it will never happen!

THE MOTHER (*recites*):

If you still live, never say: Never!
What looks certain is not certain.
The way things are will not last.
When the ruling class has spoken,
the ruled shall raise their voices.
Who dares say: Never?
Who's to blame where oppression rules? We are.
Who's responsible where the rule is smashed? We are.
Those beaten down shall rise up tall!
Whoever is lost, fights back!
Who can restrain the man who sees his situation?
The victims of today will be victors of tomorrow
And Never is changed into Today.

HOUSEMAID: A woman sixty years old carried our flag. We said to her, "Isn't the flag too heavy for you? Give us the flag!" But she said:

THE MOTHER: No; when I am tired, then I'll give it to you and you'll carry it.

FIRST WORKER: And so she marched with us, tirelessly, from the morning into the afternoon.

END

BRECHT'S NOTES TO *THE MOTHER*

I

The Mother was written in the style of a *Lehrstück* ("play for learning"), although it requires professional actors. The play's dramaturgy is anti-metaphysical, materialistic and NON-ARISTOTELIAN. Thus it declines to assist the spectator in *surrendering himself to empathy* in the unthinking fashion of the Aristotelian dramaturgy; and it relates to certain psychic effects, as for instance catharsis, in an essentially different manner: In the same way as it refuses to tacitly hand over its heroes to the world as though to an inalterable destiny, it also has no intention of handing over the spectator to a "suggestive" theater experience. Rather its concern is to teach the spectator a most definitely practical conduct that is intended to change the world, and for this reason he must be afforded a fundamentally different attitude in the theater from that to which he is accustomed. Following are several measures which were taken toward that end, during the initial production of *The Mother* in Berlin.

II

In the first production of *The Mother*   *Indirect Effect* the stage (designed by Caspar Neher)   *of the Epic Stage* was not meant to simulate an actual locality. Instead the stage itself assumed a position, as it were, in regard to the events: it quoted, recounted, anticipated, and reminded. With its sparse indications of furniture, doors, and the like, it was kept to the objects that

133

played a role; objects, that is, which, were they missing, would require the action to proceed differently or not at all. Quick scene changes were made possible by a system of solid iron pipes a little taller than a man, which were mounted vertically at varying distances about the stage, and to which could be hooked other horizontal, removable pipes of adjustable length, covered with canvas. Between these hung "practical" wooden doors in their frames. Texts and photo documents were projected onto a large canvas in the background, and these could be left on during the course of a scene so the projection linen became a backdrop as well. In this manner, through the use of texts and photo documents as well as by the indication of actual rooms, the stage showed the great intellectual movement wherein the events transpired. The projections are by no means a mere mechanical auxiliary in the sense of a "visual aid," and offer no cribsheet for the lazy. They have no intention of assisting the spectator but aim rather to oppose him; they frustrate his total empathy and interrupt his mechanical assent. They render the EFFECT INDIRECT. In this fashion they are an organic part of the work of art.

III

The Projections

Scene 1 (P. 37)

THE VLASSOVAS OF ALL NATIONS

Scene 2 (P. 40)

THE BATTLE FOR THE KOPEK
(1 Kopek = 10¢)

Scene 3 (P. 51)

Photograph: P. SUKLINOV, OWNER OF THE SUKLINOV WORKS

Scene 4 (P. 59)

THEORY TURNS INTO A MATERIAL FORCE ONCE THE MASSES HAVE UNDERSTOOD IT! *(Marx)*

Scene 5 (P. 66)

THE FIRST OF MAY. WORKERS OF ALL LANDS, UNITE!

Scene 6 (P. 71)

FOR PELAGEA VLASSOVA, OF TVER, A MEMBERSHIP CARD IN THE RUSSIAN SOCIAL-DEMOCRATIC PARTY

Scene 6 (P. 76)

THE WORKING CLASS PURSUES KNOWLEDGE, WHICH IT NEEDS FOR ITS VICTORY *(Lenin)*

Scene 7 (P. 85)

PROVE THAT YOU CAN FIGHT!

(Lenin, to the women)

Scene 8 (P. 90)

The hammer-and-sickle, not crossed as is usual, but the one beside the other, connected by the word "and."

Scene 8 (P. 93)

The hammer-and-sickle emblem: hammer and sickle are now lashed together in the usual manner.

Scene 9 (P. 99)

THE SOCIAL INVOLVEMENT OF WOMEN IS TO BE SOUGHT, SO THEY WILL LAY ASIDE THEIR PHILISTINE HOME-AND-FAMILY PSYCHOLOGY   *(Lenin)*

Scene 10 (P. 106)

PROVE THAT YOU CAN FIGHT!

(Lenin, to the women)

Scene 11 (P. 110)

RELIGION IS THE OPIUM OF THE PEOPLE   *(Marx)*

Scene 12 (P. 119)

1914. AGAINST THE CURRENT!

Scene 13 (P. 122)

Photograph of the war leaders: the Tsar, the German Kaiser, Poincaré, Wilson, Grey.

Scene 14 (P. 124)

Photograph of Lenin; beside it: TRANSFORM THE IMPERIALIST WAR INTO A CIVIL WAR

Scene 15 (P. 130)

1917

Scene 15 (P. 131 as Finale)

THE RUSSIAN PROLETARIAT SEIZED POWER IN NO-VEMBER 1917

A poster in the Auditorium:

WITHOUT THE WOMEN THERE CAN BE NO GENUINE MASS MOVEMENT   *(Lenin)*

IV

The Epic Theatre makes use of the simplest conceivable block-ing, whatever serves to render the meaning of the events clear. No attempt is made to achieve "accidental," "lifelike," or "unplanned" groupings; the stage does not mirror the "natural" disorder of things. The desired opposite of natural disorder is natural order. The ordering perspective will be of a social-historical sort. The standpoint that the director should assume is not wholly defined, though many will find it more compre-hensible, if we speak of him as a depictor of morals and an historian. The second scene of *The Mother* contains the following external happenings, which the director ought to bring out and differentiate from one another:

Epic Performance Methods

1. For the first time the young worker Pavel Vlassov is visited by his revolutionary comrades, who wish to carry out some illegal work in his home.

2. His mother is distressed to see him in the company of revolutionary workers. She tries to get rid of them.

3. As they undertake their illegal work the worker Masha Kalatova sings a brief song explaining how the workers, if they are to conquer bread and work for themselves, must "take the state and turn it over, bottoms up."

4. A house search by the police shows the mother just how dangerous is her son's new activity.

5. The mother is shocked by the police brutality, but she nevertheless declares that her son, rather than the state, is the violent one. On this basis she condemns him, and, more harshly still, his seducers.

6. The mother sees that her son has been chosen for the dangerous task of distributing leaflets. To keep him out of it she volunteers to go herself.

7. After consulting briefly the revolutionaries turn the leaflets over to her. She is unable to read them.

These seven happenings are to be performed without a trace of pathos, as momentously and strikingly as though they were well-known historical happenings. In this Epic Theatre which serves a non-Aristotelian dramaturgy, the actor will therefore have to make every effort to situate himself so he noticeably stands *between* the onlooker and the happening. This matter of MAKING NOTICEABLE, too, contributes to the wished-for indirectness of effect.

V

An Example: Description of the First Performance of The Mother

Following is something of what the first performer of the Mother, Helene Weigel, managed to show by means of Epic acting:

1. In the first scene, standing at stage center in a distinct and typical attitude, the actress

spoke her lines as though they actually had been written in the third person. Thus she avoided counterfeiting that she really was Mrs. Vlassova or thought she was and so was speaking the lines in all reality, and she moreover deterred the spectator from believing, because of carelessness or old habit, that he had been transported into a particular room as an invisible eyewitness and eavesdropper on a unique and intimate scene. Instead she openly presented the character to the spectator, as a personage he would see acting and acted upon for the coming several hours.

2. Vlassova's efforts to get rid of the revolutionaries were presented by the actress in such a manner that we might glimpse, if we were attentive, her own amusement. More terrified than forceful were her reproaches to the revolutionaries. Filled with reproach was her offer to distribute the leaflets.

3. In the manner whereby she forced her way into the factory yard, she demonstrated what a fine catch the revolutionaries would get should they win such a fighter to their side.

4. She receives her first instruction in Communism with the demeanor of a great realist. She does battle with her discussion opponents with a certain friendly energy— as if they were idealists incapable of seeing reality for what it is. She requires not only that a proof be true, but that it be plausible as well.

5. The May Day demonstration was spoken as though those concerned stood before the bar of justice. At its end the performer of Smilgin manifested the defeat by going down on one knee, whereupon the performer of the Mother bent forward and with her final words took up the flag he had let fall.

6. From this point on the Mother was presented as considerably more friendly and thoughtful; except for the very start of these scenes, when she looked as though in shock. The "Praise of Communism" was sung quietly and gently.

The scene in which the Mother learns to read and write in company with other workers, is among the most difficult for the performer. Spectator laughter at individual lines must not distract the actor from showing the learning difficulties of elderly and inflexible people. The seriousness of a genuinely historical event must be achieved: for here occurs the socialization of knowledge, the intellectual expropriation of the bourgeoisie by a proletariat long exploited and relegated to menial labor. This happening does not emerge "between the lines," it is directly stated. Whenever something is directly said in a scene, a number of our actors begin restlessly to cast about for something they might indirectly represent. They seize upon "something ineffable" between the lines that is solely dependent upon *them*. Because this conduct renders the expressible and expressed banal, it is harmful.

In the brief scene "Ivan Vessovchikov Fails to Recognize his Brother," the performer gave expression to the Mother's belief that the Teacher did not possess any inalterable essence. But she avoided laying her finger upon the changes intended.

7. The Mother must accomplish her revolutionary work under the enemy's very eyes. She deceives the Guard by appearing like the archetypal white-haired mother with her conversation disjointed and memory-provoking. She awakens in the Guard a sympathy which ends by disarming him. Thus she makes excellent use of her intimate knowledge of the old type of mother love which is exhausted; she is herself the example of a new and effective variety. The performer showed that the Mother was aware of the humor in the situation.

8. In this scene too the actress showed that Vlassova, as well as she, merrily enjoys the light comedy of impersonation. She made clear her conviction that the Estate Butcher could be awakened to his class allegiances only by a passive if flexible behavior, that the tone of one

injured with good cause had to suffice. She performed the small and modest drop that fills the cup to overflowing. The "Praise of the Vlassovas" (an example of curbing praise) was recited before the curtain, with Vlassova present and standing somewhat to the side.

11. The Mother's grief for her son may be indicated by having her hair white from this point on. Her grief, though profound, is only hinted. It certainly does not destroy her sense of humor, with which the account of God's evaporation should be imbued.

12. In this case the actress placed herself against the workers with whom she spoke, but she also showed herself one of them. Thus taken together, she and they conveyed the image of the proletariat at the time when war broke out. The "y-y-yess" which occurs at the start of the scene's last speech was particularly spoken with special care, and it very nearly became the chief effect in the scene. Starting in the stooped attitude (of an old woman) the actress lifted her chin and smiled; the word came forth in a soft drawn-out falsetto, as if to say she understood the seductions of saying the hell with everything, but understood as well the need for everyone sharing the proletariat's situation to perform their utmost from that point on.

14. The actress made her anti-war propaganda by starting out stooped, her head averted and concealed in a large head scarf through which she spoke. She manifested the mole-like skill required by the work.

In every situation she chose, from all the possible traits, those which, if acquired, would enable the Vlassovas to carry their political action into the broadest sphere (they were thus also quite individual, unique and particular!) and those which would enable the Vlassovas to carry out their work themselves; thus she performed as it were before a gathering of political persons, though she was for all that no less the actress, nor did she perform without art.

VI

In order to combat the spectator's "involve-   *Choruses*
ment," his "free" associations, small choruses
can be located in the auditorium to place before him the
correct attitude and invite him to form opinions, draw upon
his experience, and practice self-control. These choruses
will direct an APPEAL TO THE PRACTICAL MAN IN THE
SPECTATOR; they will call him to emancipate himself from
the world as it is presented, and from the presentation too.
Following are some examples of texts for the choruses.
They should be considered alterable (according to the situation), and may be augmented or replaced by the reading
of quotations or documents or by the delivery of songs.

SCENE ONE

*P. 37, after: "Early morning: The Mother cooks soup for
her son who is going to work."*

FIRST CHORUS:

See this mother and son! Alienation
has come between them. Through outside circumstance
she becomes all but his enemy. You witness here
the battle of the friendly mother and her hostile son.
Plainly is it seen
how the battle raging outside cannot be kept from this room,
and no one escapes unharmed from the field swarming
        with battle.

P. 37, after: "He just gets more and more discontented."

SECOND CHORUS:

His discontent comes from having seen his situation!

And the entire world
waits upon his discontent.

P. 38, after: "I see nothing to be done."

THIRD CHORUS:

Just see how far she is still
from seeing her task, her immense task! She still wonders
how to dispose of his shrinking wages, so he
can live on still less, thanks to her quiet skill!

SCENE TWO

P. 41, after: "I don't set out tea for such people."

FOURTH CHORUS:

The mother believes her natural enemy
are those strengthening her son in his revolt. She would
be glad, were her son still sweet-tempered,
still gladly seen by his oppressors, for then
he might somehow elude the misery, and possibly
make his way among the exploiters. Nothing but
danger can greet these efforts to improve his shelter—
even such shelter as this!

*P. 46, after: "They do not do the right thing. But he isn't
doing the right thing, either."*

FIFTH CHORUS:

Hold it! Stop here! She shows us astonishing things.
Here she condemns her enemy as cruel. But she calls

only the practice cruel, and not its legality!
Some other people condemn the law that is cruel, and
forgive those who practice it. Both ways are wrong! The law
cannot be detached from those who serve it, nor
the state from its rulers!
It is no more just than they! For men
have made it. From men it comes forth, for men
is it planned,
but not for all men
for only the few and these are not you.
How quickly the rumor gets around, and how long it lasts
saying the state is different from those who run it
more noble than those using it for their own good.
It is said they are good people in a bad job, or we hear talk
they are bad people serving a good cause.
But in truth
he is bad who acts badly, and the cause of bad people is bad.
So never say the state is good that treats you badly,
don't say it could be better. No. Were it better
there would be no more state.

SCENE THREE

P. 57, after: "He is so discontented already."

SIXTH CHORUS:

Look: at last she notices: It is my cause too,
and the struggle is useful. Soon
she will fight. Soon she will be ready
to say loudly: This battle is useful
in a loud firm voice: For me especially!

VII

It was not to be avoided that spectators habituated to their usual "experience" would have their difficulties:

Is non-Aristotelian dramaturgy of the Type of The Mother *Primitive?*

ACHT-UHR-ABENDBLATT, 1/18/1932

". . . Brecht appealed to the ear and the reason. He almost wholly omitted the supportative Russian milieu and psychology, which in Gorki's depiction had turned a propaganda work into an artwork . . ."

DEUTSCHE ZEITUNG, BERLIN, 1/18/1932

". . . Actors are at hand, suited to the style of these productions, who captivate with the clarity of their acting. We are forced to add that the true acting art, by which we mean passion transformed into the play witnessed upon the stage, is suppressed. In its place we find the messenger bearing information, the storyteller, and the disinterested spectator."

WESTFÄLISCHER KURIER, HAMM

". . . He (Billinger) shows also in his conclusion how one soul, after the downfall of this demon-seduced couple during the press of events and excited by the Grace of the Lord's Day, one soul, drawn in the wake of the couple during the wild night, decides upon the path of Honor. —It is Billinger's masterstroke, the way in which he figures this all forth in the name of Honor just as the Mystery of God's Incarnation and the Holy Family has covertly figured it forth to us. We are indeed proud to know a Catholic dramatist is finally being performed again in such a prominent place.

"In contrast, how poor a work is *The Mother* as performed by a Communistic group of young actors and dramatized by Brecht as a *Lehrstück* based upon the well-known novel by Maxim Gorki. The experiences of a worker's wife who no longer has enough to eat for her son, are developed systematically from private life and into the Party, with the intention of proving that the Mother's place also is there where, according to the teaching of Lenin, the imperialist war will be transformed into civil war."

DEUTSCHE TAGESZEITUNG, 1/18/1932

". . . What took place up to the moment when the eyes of the public strayed elsewhere, is devastatingly arid and childish . . ."

DER VORWÄRTS, BERLIN, 1/18/1932

". . . It (Gorki's novel) is a magnificent novel. . . . Pelagea is permitted to die as a proletarian soul fully deserving of adoration, though the gendarmes of the Tsar hound this shining revolutionary to her death . . .
". . . But Brecht overturns the wonderful Gorkyism of that time, turning it into the Stalinism of 1932 . . .
". . . In brief, the transformation of this splendid novel into a drama makes it once more a novel, but lacking the psychological luster."

BERLINER TAGEBLATT, 1/18/1932

". . . It remains to be said, in the spirit of mitigating friendliness, that here is a play for primitive audiences. But then, it is the work of a primitive author."

It is easily seen how the bourgeois public stubbornly insists upon the prompt satisfaction of its ideological and nerve-soothing theater demands. Should the theater not measure up to its requisite function, or fail in part, then the theater has failed entirely and is too arid or primitive. To see the extreme difficulty of shattering these rigid definitions of function, one must look at the naive confession of Andor Gabor in *Linkskurve,* which appears in a discussion of production methods by (alleged) followers of the Epic Theatre in connection with Becher's *The Great Plan.* Gabor writes:

LINKSKURVE, *Nov.-Dec.* 1932

"Even if he (the spectator) went with the intention of cheering the stage, authors and performers, he could not do it. What was presented 'only'—this is no little—tightened the strings. It failed to bring forth the resounding melody that all one's nerves cried out for."

Thus do even the politically enlightened people sometimes respond! And in all the rest of the discussion, not one line concerning the political results of the affair! Even so, only through the spectator's unusually strong interest in politics, or in default of that then his interest in philosophy or practical conduct, can the theater be led toward a new social function. Accordingly the workers who saw *The Mother* could not but have left the performance of the play richer in experience. Nor could they find the play primitive.

WELT AM ABEND, 1/18/1932

". . . Actually it is not a primitive genre. There were in fact numerous scenes upon which entire courses of discussion could be based."

Not even for a moment did these spectators believe that what they saw described a particular historical occurrence in Russia, to the end that they might "participate vicariously" in an adventure that would "bring the eternally human into focus," etc. They were as far from wishing to forget the inhuman conditions, very particular and alterable, under which they live. Rather these spectators were ready to mobilize all their experience and intelligence and combative spirit, so to recognize problems and tasks, to make comparisons, to raise objections, and to criticize the conduct of the stage personages or, growing more abstract, to make applications to their own situations and from that to learn. This was a psychology they could understand; it is an APPLIED AND POLITICAL PSYCHOLOGY. The spectator is dealt with as a person who confronts depictions of human beings the prototypes of which he must deal with himself in reality (by bringing them to make avowals and undertake actions). It is for this reason that the depictions must not be taken for strictly determined phenomena. The task of the spectator, in confrontation with his fellow man, consists of interjecting himself among the determining factors. The dramaturgy is obligated to aid him in this task. For this reason the determining factors such as the social milieu, special occurrences, etc., are to be presented as alterable. A sort of "interchangeable" quality in the occurrences and circumstances must help the spectator to assemble, experiment and abstract for himself, and to make this his task. Of the many differences among individuals, those of interest to the POLITICAL person—who must have concourse with them, commence from them, combat them—are very particular differences, for instance those which when known make the conduct of the class struggle an easier matter. The political person fails to see the point of taking a definite human being and stripping him of all particularities until he stands naked, "the" Human Being, thus a being not to be altered. Rather the human being must be apprehended in his uniqueness as a portion of the fate of all human beings (and the spectator). The definition of man must be practical.

When we speak of having a "mental grip" (*Begreifen*) on what constitutes a human being, we certainly mean no less than: having some kind of hold (*Griffe*) on him. That "total" view of man, which outlines him for us and is momentarily necessary, nevertheless is inadequate save as an hypothesis for the real and decisive operation of getting a "mental grip," which *manipulates* him, and for just that purpose requires a "total" view as a kind of situational plan. But even this "total" view is not to be gained without some sort of operational plan; only in conjunction with this can the view be gained and made effective. We can obtain a mental grip on what constitutes another only when we get some sort of hold (*eingreifen*) on him. Even with ourselves, we have a mental grip on ourselves only when we "have hold of" ourselves (*eingreifen*). The human being appears to be above all a creature used by and useful to human beings, not yet defined to an end. Or in any case it is practical for the Communist organization, the organization that must fight the perverted usage of man by man, to so define him. Thus defined, he appears beyond all his tractability in his totality —as unexpectedly as this may happen.

VIII

The prevailing aesthetic requires of an artwork that it have a "direct" effect. In making this demand, it demands also that the effect bridge all social and other distinctions among individuals. A similar, class-bridging effect is also sought by the plays still written today in the Aristotelian style of dramaturgy, even though individuals are becoming increasingly aware of class distinctions. This effect is sought even when the subject of these dramas

The "Direct,"
Bridging Effect

is class contradictions, and even when the play takes its stand for one or another class. In every case a collective community is engendered in the auditorium *for the duration of the aesthetic enjoyment,* on the basis of this "universally human" of which the entire audience partakes. The manufacture of this collective community holds no interest for a non-Aristotelian dramaturgy on the order of *The Mother.* Rather it splits its public.

NEUE PREUSSISCHE KREUZZEITUNG, BERLIN, 1/18/1932

". . . It concerns a mother who is drawn into Party work by her son until at last she becomes a sturdy hand at boring from within for Communism. Hence, a song of uplift for the little man within the Party who does his duty. Crude, inflammatory, propagandistically conceived. For the True Believers, a real festival, more powerful than speeches or newspapers. To the outsider, a madness . . ."

IX

DEUTSCHE ALLGEMEINE ZEITUNG, BERLIN, 1/17/1932

". . . In this dramatic adaptation of Maxim Gorki's novel *Mother,* Brecht once more has written a *Lehrstück* that guides primitive audiences toward the correct, i.e., Communist behavior in every phase of living. As theater and as literature it is dreadful. But as political propaganda, one must pay heed to it . . .

Is Communism Exclusive?

". . . Political conduct is the theme of the play; its goal is to bring the onlooker to embrace it. This goal is so knowingly pursued by every means that the politically-minded will find much more of interest in this production than will people like ourselves, when, as surely must happen, this work is guided through the meeting halls of the North and East . . .

"We encounter with no pleasure this tale of the mother who is drawn into Communism by her son and his friends despite her resistance, only to undertake on her own an energetic Communistic propaganda. The authors had no poetic intentions, nothing but purely political goals . . ."

GERMANIA, BERLIN, 1/19/1932

". . . at last we are able to reply to those who view Brecht as an aesthetic phenomenon—just because he allegedly invented a new style of theater.

"Behind him stands no trace of his individual will. Nor of formal intentions. Behind him stands—as this evening of theater proved!—the entire Communistic ideology. It stands behind Brecht, as behind a playwright who has slowly evolved himself into one of Bolshevism's literary interpreters in Germany. In the event he becomes somebody whom one no longer evaluates in aesthetic, but rather in *political* terms."

KÖNIGSBERGER ALLGEMEINE ZEITUNG, 2/23/1932

"Poetry has nothing to do with this tale of the mother who is drawn into Communism by her son and his friends despite her resistance, only to undertake on her own an energetic Communistic propaganda. It is purely a play with a message, very well fashioned by methods that Brecht has derived from his principles of the Epic Theatre."

DEUTSCHE ALLGEMEINE ZEITUNG, BERLIN, 1/17/1932

". . . Theatrically it is, all of it, inconsequential; the work is political, it hammers away at Only Force Will

Work, and All Means are Proper and Important . . .
". . . Because the means are not the end, there is little
to be said concerning the theatrical aspects . . ."

GERMANIA, BERLIN, 1/19/1932

"The entire thing is a simple, direct and clear glorifica-
tion of a revolutionary sort of woman, led out of the
bourgeoisie into the world of proletarian class conflict."

DEUTSCHE ALLGEMEINE ZEITUNG, BERLIN, 1/17/1932

". . . The political content of this *Lehrstück* is not to
be underrated, merely because its mental effect is so dulling
and enervating . . .
". . . For the propaganda here is at the same time the
practical guide to conduct—and that is the decisive factor."

NEUE LEIPZIGER ZEITUNG

". . . There is but one single un-bourgeois element in
all the world, and that is the Free Spirit. *The Mother,* by
Brecht, just like all theatrical propaganda presentations of
an organized revolution, reeks of solid petit-bourgeois
homeliness."   (H. Kesten)

Most if not all the bourgeois critics of *The Mother* told
us the same thing: this was a presentation only for Communists. They spoke as though it were like something
for rabbit breeders, or chess players, which could not
interest many people and above all could not be judged
by those who know nothing of rabbits or chess. And yet,
though all the world may not feel itself concerned with
Communism, Communism is concerned with all the world.
Communism is no private enclave among other private
enclaves. It proceeds radically on the basis of abolishing

private property among the means of production; and it opposes all tendencies, regardless of how they are differentiated from one another, which continue to agree on the retention of private property. It declares that the direct and sole way to continue our great Western philosophy, is to provide that continuance by means of radically revising that philosophy's function. Similarly the only practical continuation, it says, of the Western (capitalist) development and therewith, the radical revision of the attained economy, lies in a similar direction. We should and must say in this respect, that our assertions are objective and generally binding, not subjective and limited. We are speaking not for ourselves as a tiny segment of mankind, but for the whole of mankind, as the segment that represents the interests of the whole (not a segment) of mankind. Let nobody conclude that we are not objective, simply because we are involved in struggle. Any person who today seeks to give the impression that he is not in the struggle, and seeks to suggest that he is objective, will be seen upon closer examination to represent only the interests of a tiny and hopelessly subjective segment of mankind. Objectively viewed, he will, by his favor for retaining the capitalist relations of ownership and production, be betraying the interests of the whole of mankind. The seeming-objective "leftish" bourgeois skeptic does not or will not realize that he fights in this great struggle too, at precisely the moment when he declines to call the permanent practice of power by a small elite, which goes unnoticed through long usage, a "fight." "Goods of an ideal nature" must be struck collectively from the hands of this possessing elite, which is a degenerate and filthy, objectively and subjectively inhuman *clique*. And this without first asking what a mankind exploited, frustrated in its productivity, and now defending itself against the decay of mankind, may then wish to do with the goods. This elite must be declared forfeit of all claim to human respect— prior to, and regardless of what else is done. Whatever may be meant in the future by freedom, justice, humanity, culture, productivity, courage, reliability, these words must no longer be used until the concepts are purified of all that their functioning in bourgeois society has attached to them. Our opponents are the opponents of mankind. They are not "right" from their own point of view, rather the wrong subsists in their point of view. Perhaps they have to be as they are, but they do not have to be. It is understandable that they defend themselves, but what they defend is theft and privilege and to understand must not mean to excuse. Whosoever is a wolf to man is a wolf, not a man. Today, as the bare self-defense of the great masses turns into the final struggle for power, "kindness" comes to mean the annihilation of those who make kindness impossible.

GERMANIA, BERLIN, 1/19/1932

"*The Mother* is thus the evolution of a person from the sphere of private human affairs into the general and political sphere, in the Marxist sense. She loves her son, a worker and the son of a worker. Conflict breaks out over the kopek that is lacking for the daily soup. It ends with the red flag which the old woman, at the head of the Party, bears into demonstrations up until the 1917 revolution. Thereby she goes through all the exercises of a Communist schooling, from handbill distribution through study of the ABC's and instruction of peasants to the 'glorious' Leninist revolt. She learns to work for the Party, at first impersonally, then inhumanly, at least deceitfully (all in the Party's interest, of course), then as an agitator: at first by honorable means but later even with lies. During the war, for instance, she behaves at first as if she were courageously giving up her copper—but then, with 'bourgeois' arguments, she cunningly manages to send others homeward until at last she confesses her true colors. She favors 'transforming the imperialist war into a civil war' (Lenin) and she finally takes a part herself in the 'transformation' and its triumph,—such is the teaching of this play."

The bourgeois critics conclude that such works as this, far from arousing specific interests of a general nature, appear rather to presume concerns of much less than general nature. In point of fact the interests that are here presumed dormant, at the very least, are of a very special general kind. That is why they are opposed to the bourgeois critics' interests. For those groups of brainworkers who are linked intellectually by their existential ties to the possessors of the means of production, it is not with the cause of Communism but with the cause of the world that they no longer have any connection. Detaching themselves from the Communists as from one-sided, enchained, unfree spirits, they but detach themselves from the cause of mankind and ally themselves with exploitation—which is, we grant, universal and unfettered and freely practiced. It is undeniable that numerous brainworkers are struck by the feeling that the world (their world) is beset with contradictions. Yet they do nothing about it. And supposing we disallow those who merely construe a mental world, contradictory in the abstract (that is, existing by virtue of its contradictions), we find ourselves faced with people who may be more or less conscious of the contradictions but who nevertheless behave as though the world were in good accord. Thus, the hold of the world upon the thought of such people is imperfect; we should not be astonished that their thought has no "mental grip" upon the world. What this really means, however, is that they do not demand of their thought that it have a hold on things. From this springs the "Pure Spirit" that exists in the abstract and is only more or less hindered by "external" circumstance. Such persons find no common ground between the realm of the mind and the discussions with a working-woman which the play *The Mother* provoked. That is why they send their political experts. Just as they have no concern for practical conduct, by the same token "the others" have nothing to do with the mind. Why should the brain worry about what the hand does that fills its pockets! These people are anti-political. This means in practice that they favor the politics that will include them. Their behavior is thoroughly political, even in their professional capacities. To take up residence outside politics is not the same thing as being excluded from politics; and the person standing outside politics does not stand above politics.

A number of these people believe they can perfect themselves under the conditions of an imperfect state, without having to perfect the state. But it is a premise of our state that it cannot use fulfilled or self-perfecting people. We observe institutions on every hand that can use only cripples: those who are missing an arm, or a leg, or both legs. The administration's affairs are best carried out by mental deficients. Thugs must make up the forces of law and order, if they are to carry out their duties, and our judges must be blind. The scholars, deaf and dumb; or at least dumb. And the newspapers and book publishers, so as not to go bankrupt, count only upon illiterates. What is called Wisdom is manifested, not in the discovery and proclamation of Truth, but rather in the discovery of Falsehood and in more or less refined means of keeping it concealed. There are some who cannot see any sign of great masterpieces and ascribe this to the lack of great talents. But no Homer and no Shakespeare would be capable of putting into verse what they want to hear. Moreover, these people who detect no sign of great masterpieces will manage to get along very well without them; though, perhaps, they could not live with them.

X

A chief objection that bourgeois criticism has raised against non-Aristotelian-dramaturgy of the type of *The Mother,* is based upon a

Aversion to Learning and Contempt for the Useful

separation of the concepts of "entertaining" and "educational," which is likewise purely bourgeois. In this perspective *The Mother* is thought possibly educational (though it is, as said earlier, for but a small segment of the possible audience), but it certainly is not entertaining (even to the small segment). Let us probe into this dichotomy. Are we astonished to note that what is intended is a denigration pure and simple of learning when it is not presented as enjoyment? In truth, of course, it is enjoyment that is denigrated whenever scrupulously deprived of all its instructive worth. Let us but examine the function lent to learning within the bourgeois social organization. It functions as a purchase of knowledge that can be turned to material profit. The purchase is obligatory, before the individual is allowed to enter the system of production. Thus its place is in the sphere of the immature. Supposing I do not yet know some subject that is important in my specialization, then I'll not be willing to let myself get caught learning. For this is equivalent to admitting that my skills are less than competitive and I cannot get credit. Such frightful memories as these pursue people who come into the theater for their "entertainment"; they recall how children of the bourgeoisie get "knowledge" drummed into their heads, and they do not mean ever again to let themselves be treated like a person "seated on the schoolbench." Thus is the attitude of learning defamed.

In a similar way the useful, and a sense for the useful, have been treated to contempt ever since man began to use himself only in vile ways, for the reason that use could be further derived only from the utilization of our fellow men.

Useful is the man who can be utilized and is without rights. But before a man will make himself useful the breadbasket must be drawn a little higher above him. He who utilizes him, too, now ceases to obtain self-respect from the usage, and he turns to obtaining it from material and cultural purchases that were made possible by the usages he has drawn upon (and drawn upon in darkness). We have with us still the gesture of feudal personages who, fully assured of their prerogatives, pretend they need not use themselves nor others. We have inherited, from the time of the petit-bourgeoisie's submission, a contempt for the self-sufficient producer who uses no other man than himself; it is the contempt of capitalists who surpass him by using others in production. And, as we can see from the banishment of the act of utilization to the status of a crime committed in darkness, announcement is already made of the gigantic disturbance of the ideological systems that will be effected by the oppressed and rising proletariat. There grows at the same time in the proletariat a new, boundless and forceful sense of the useful, a sense that can breed no scruples for the reason that it aims to extirpate those relationships which have based use upon harm.